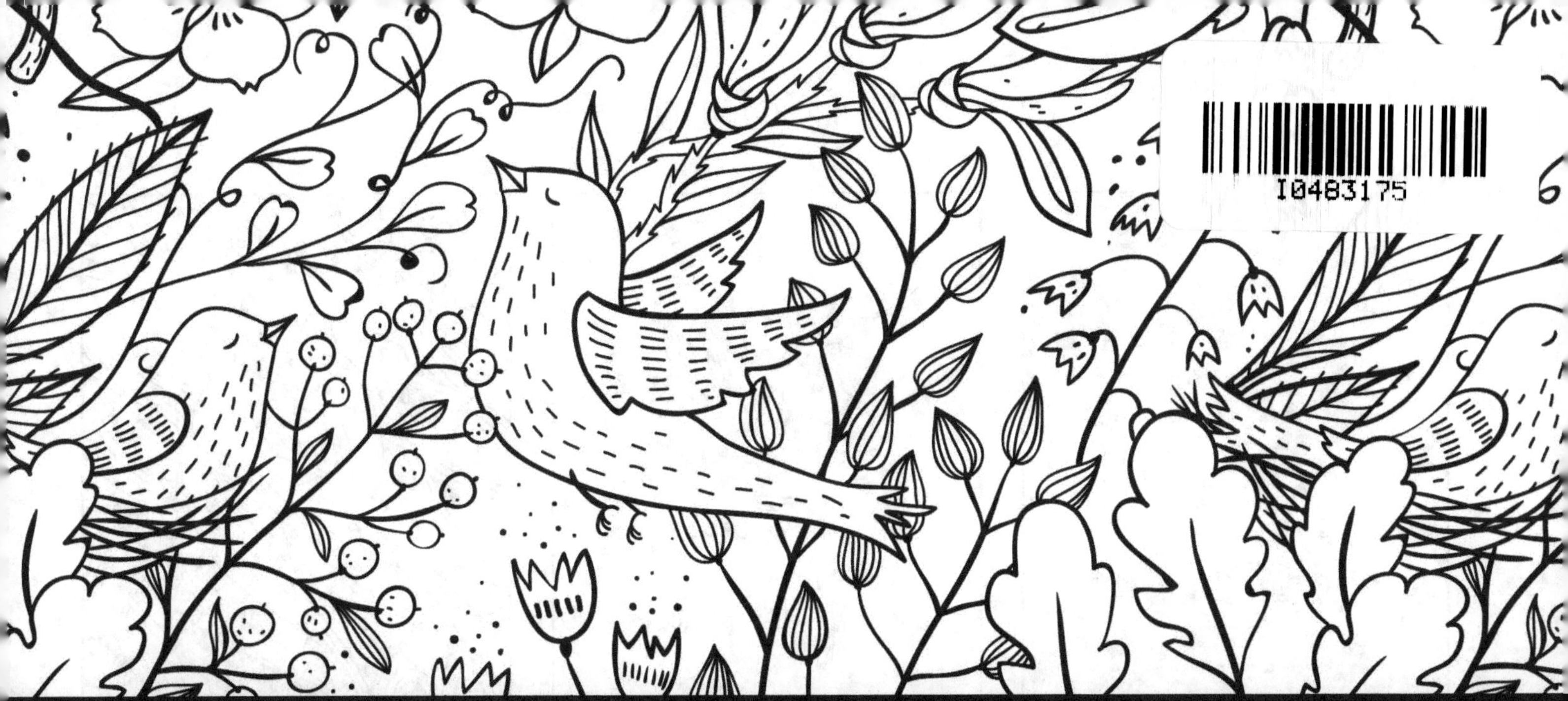

COLORING BOOKS
FOR TEEN GIRLS VOL 2
DETAILED DESIGNS

ART THERAPY COLORING

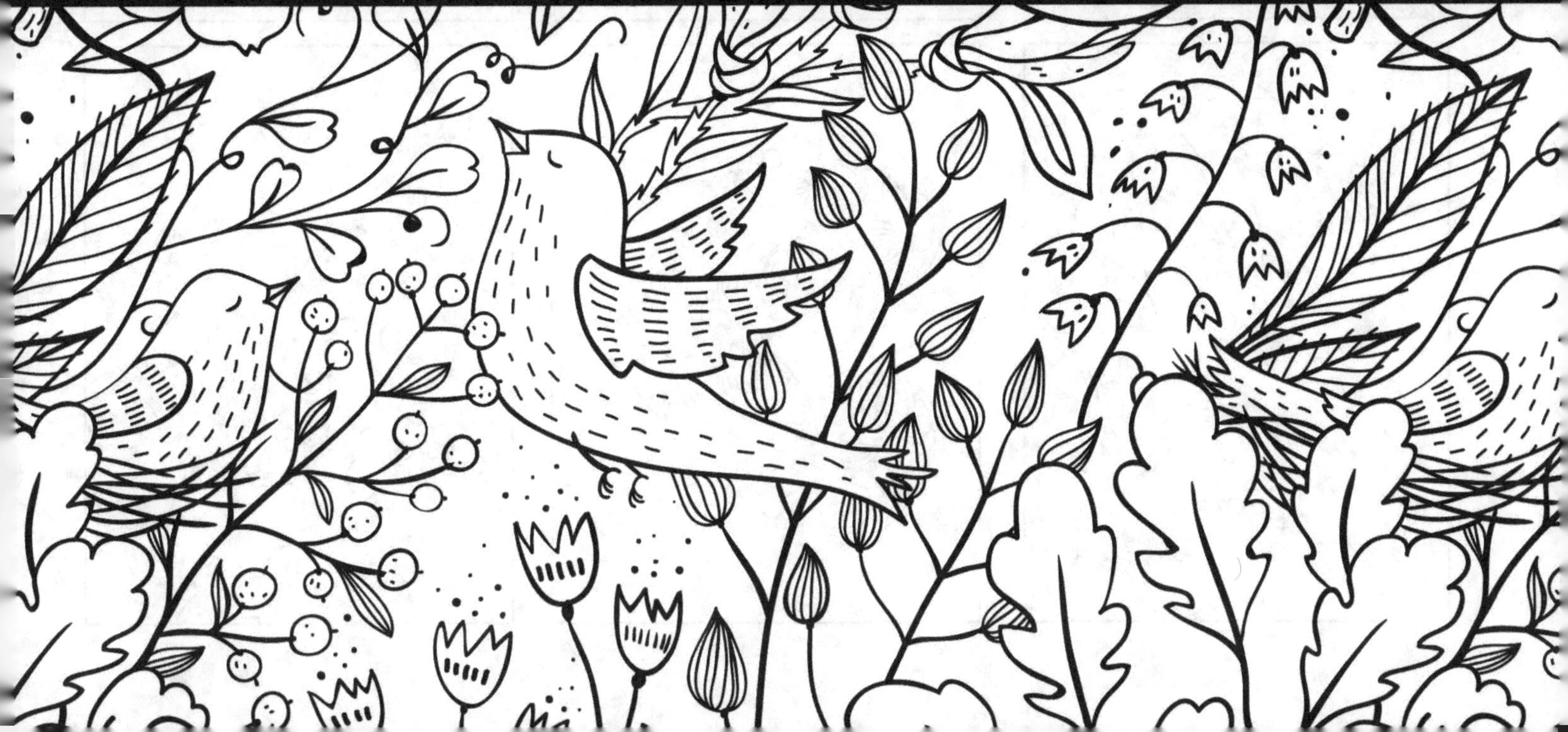

Preview of Coloring Pages

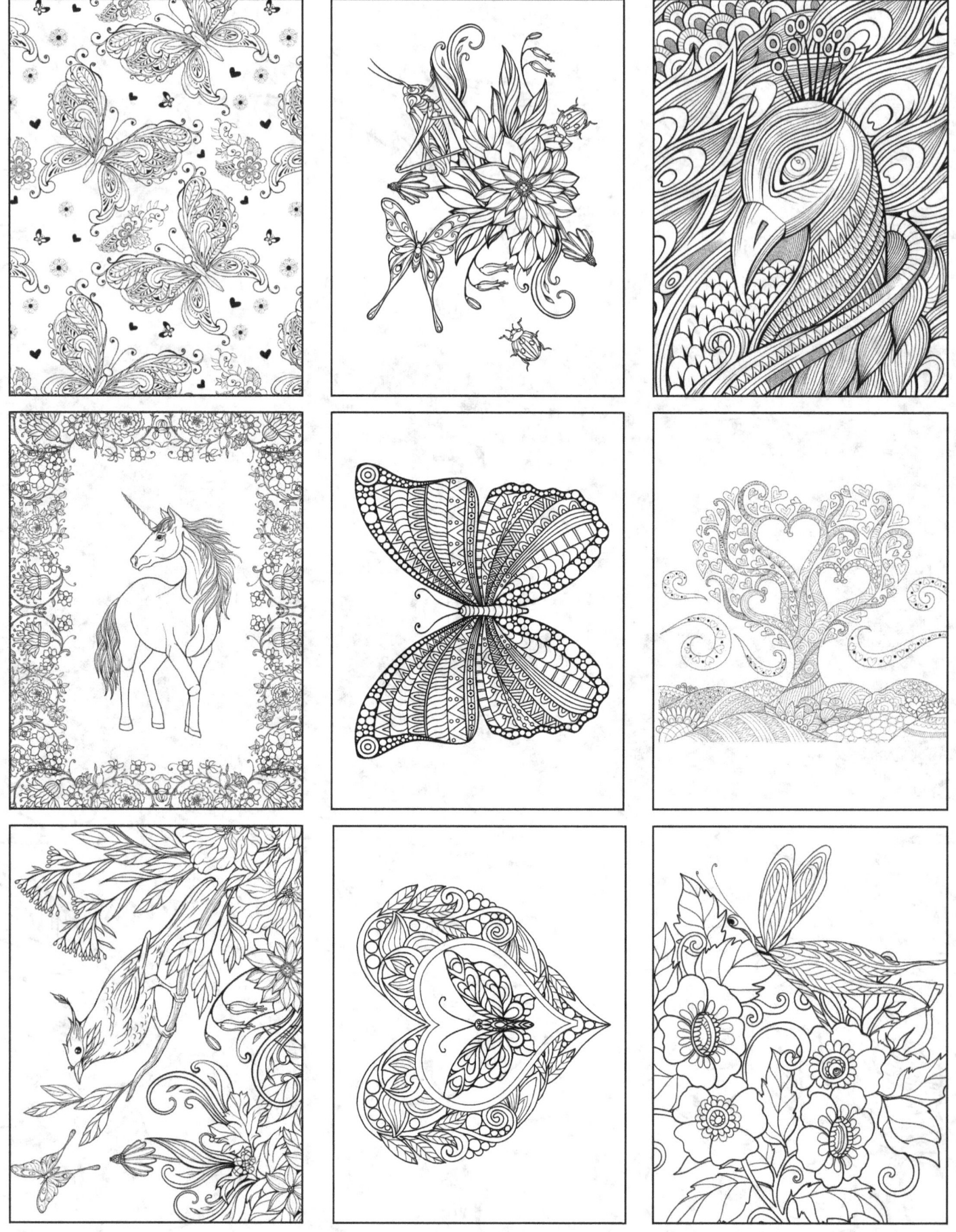

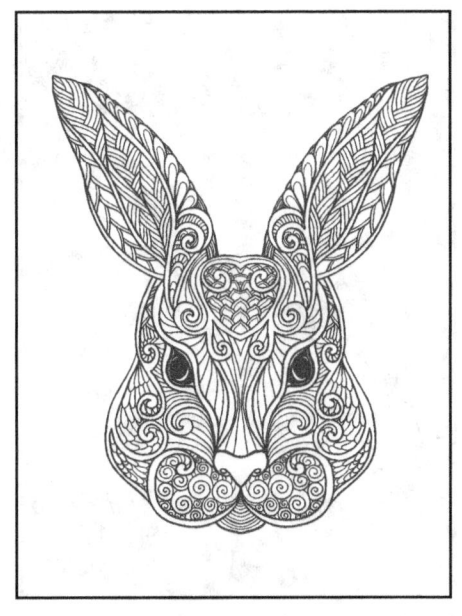
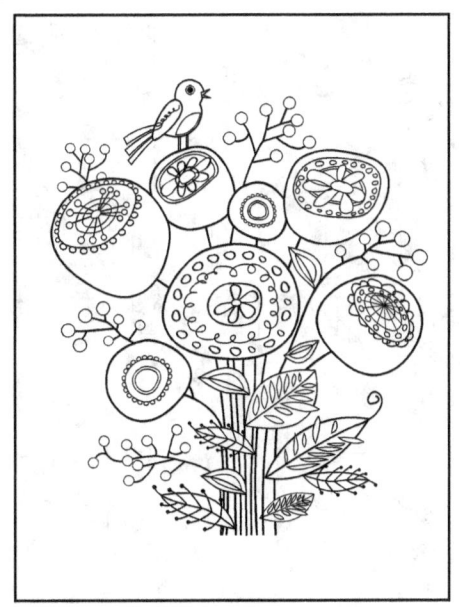
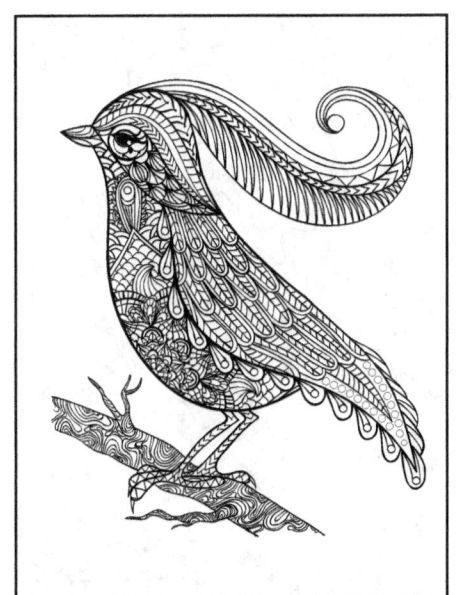
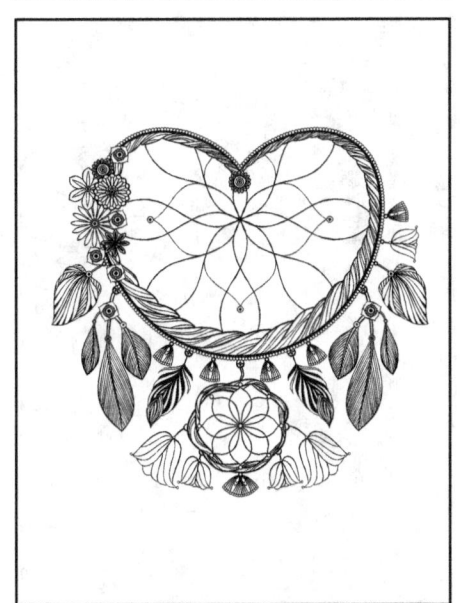
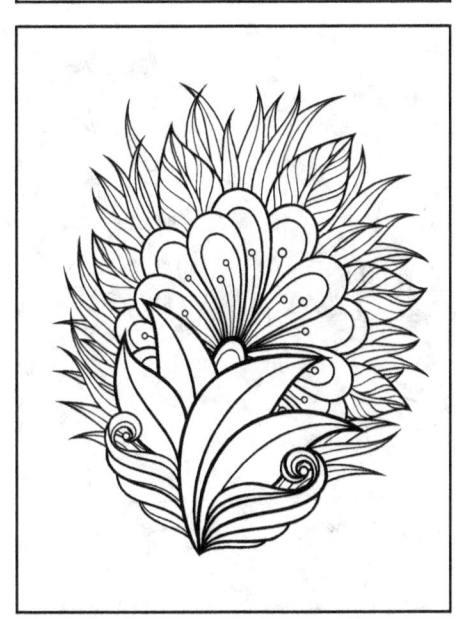
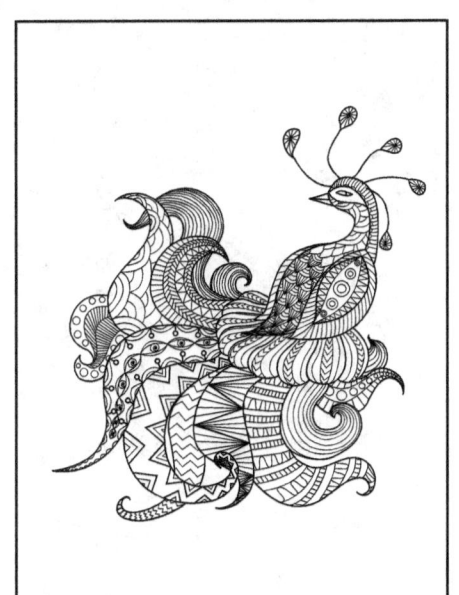
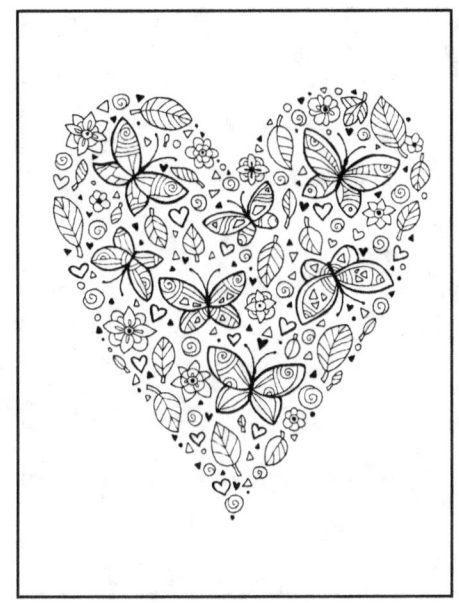
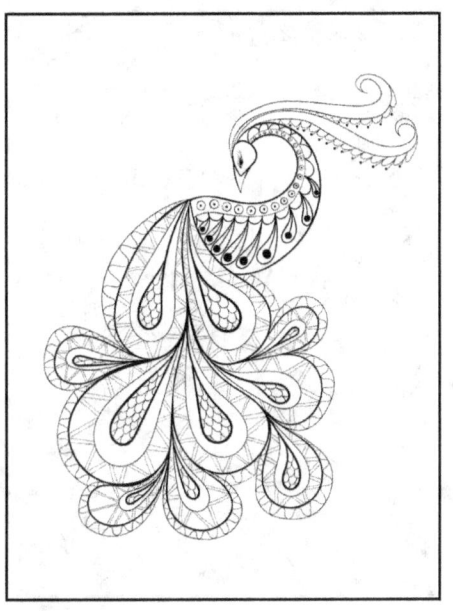
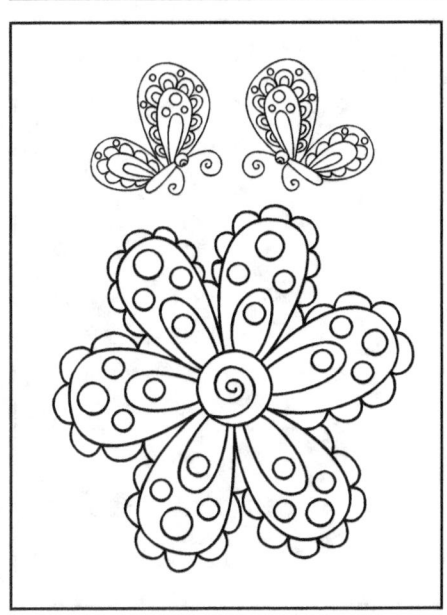

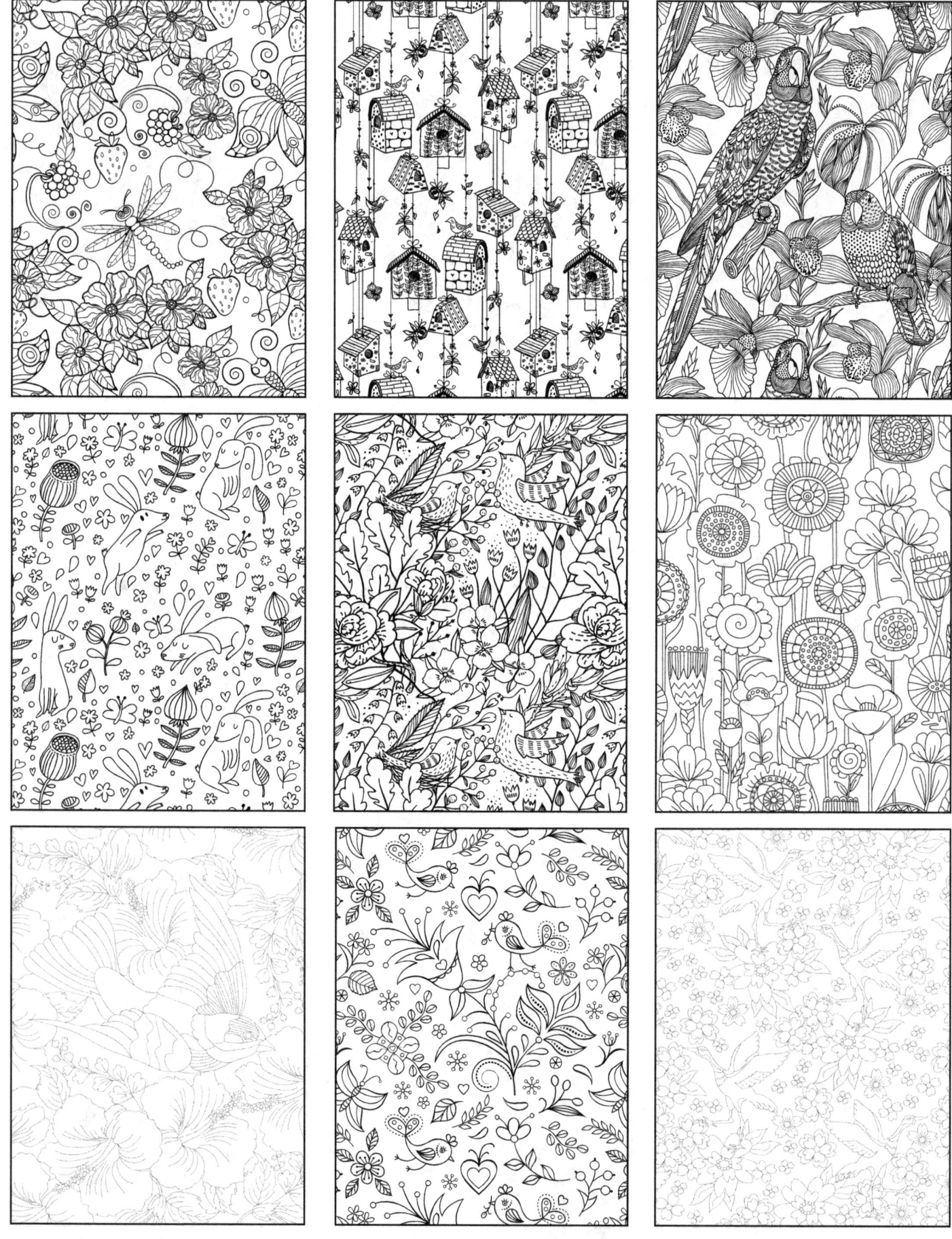

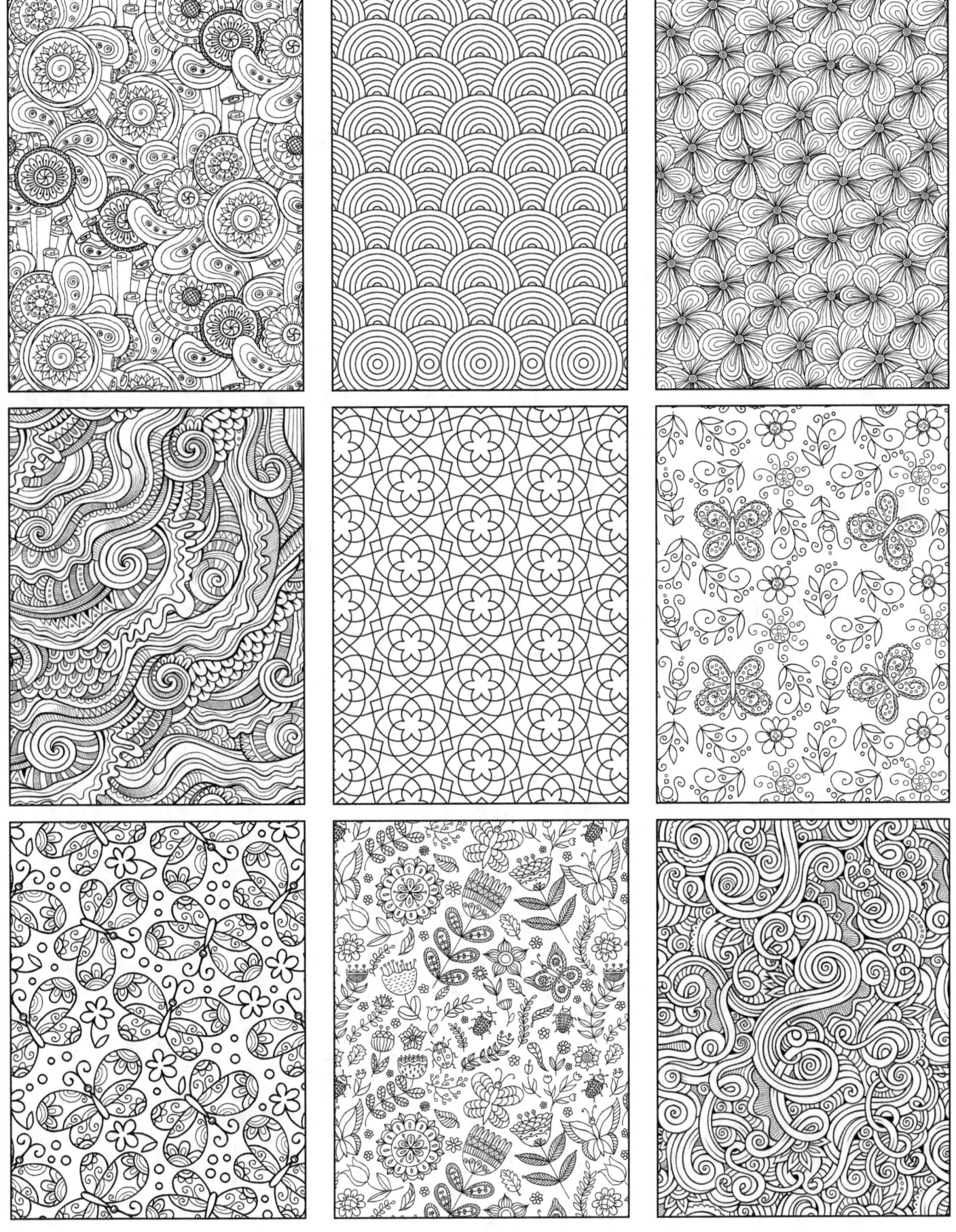

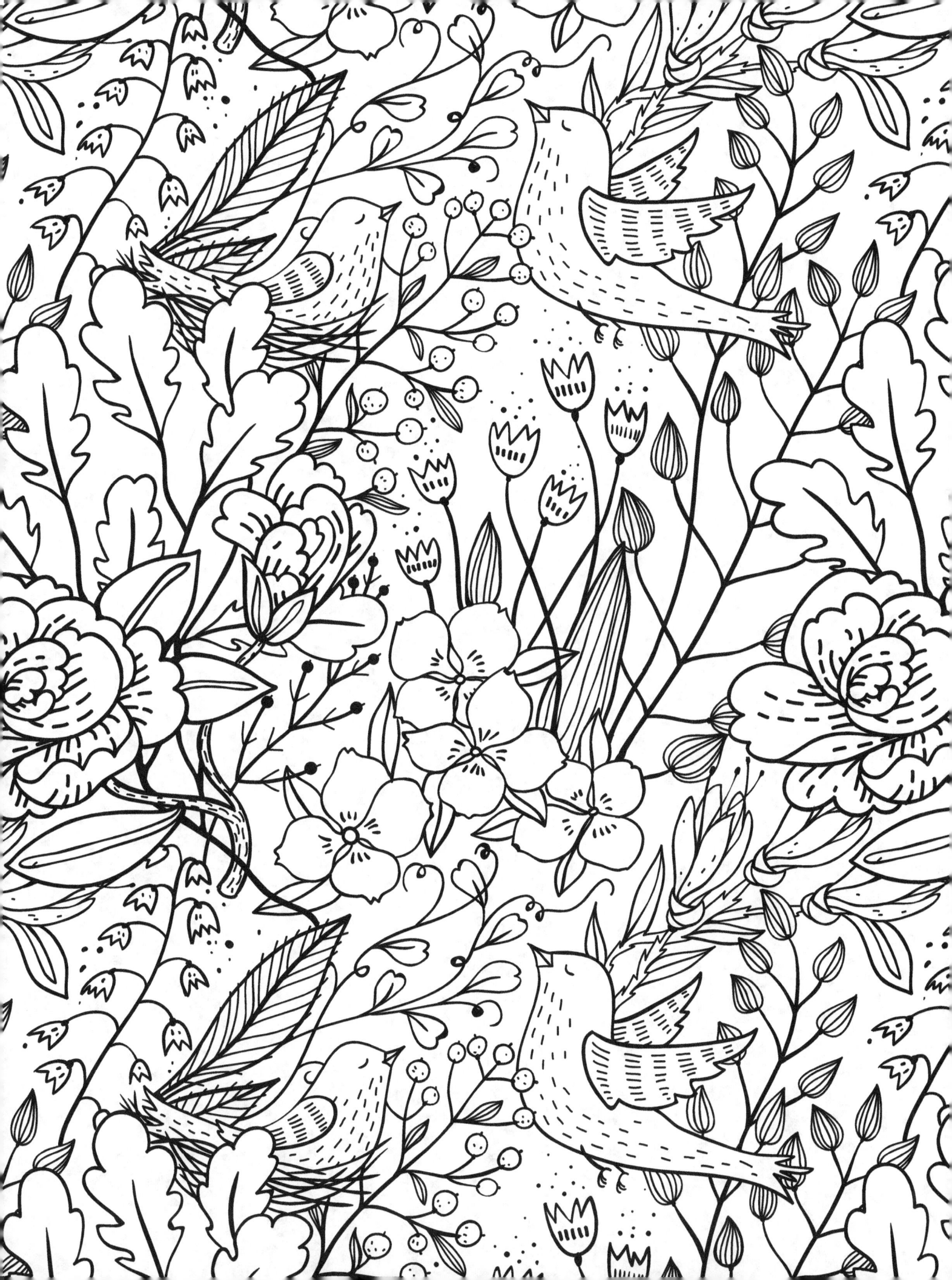

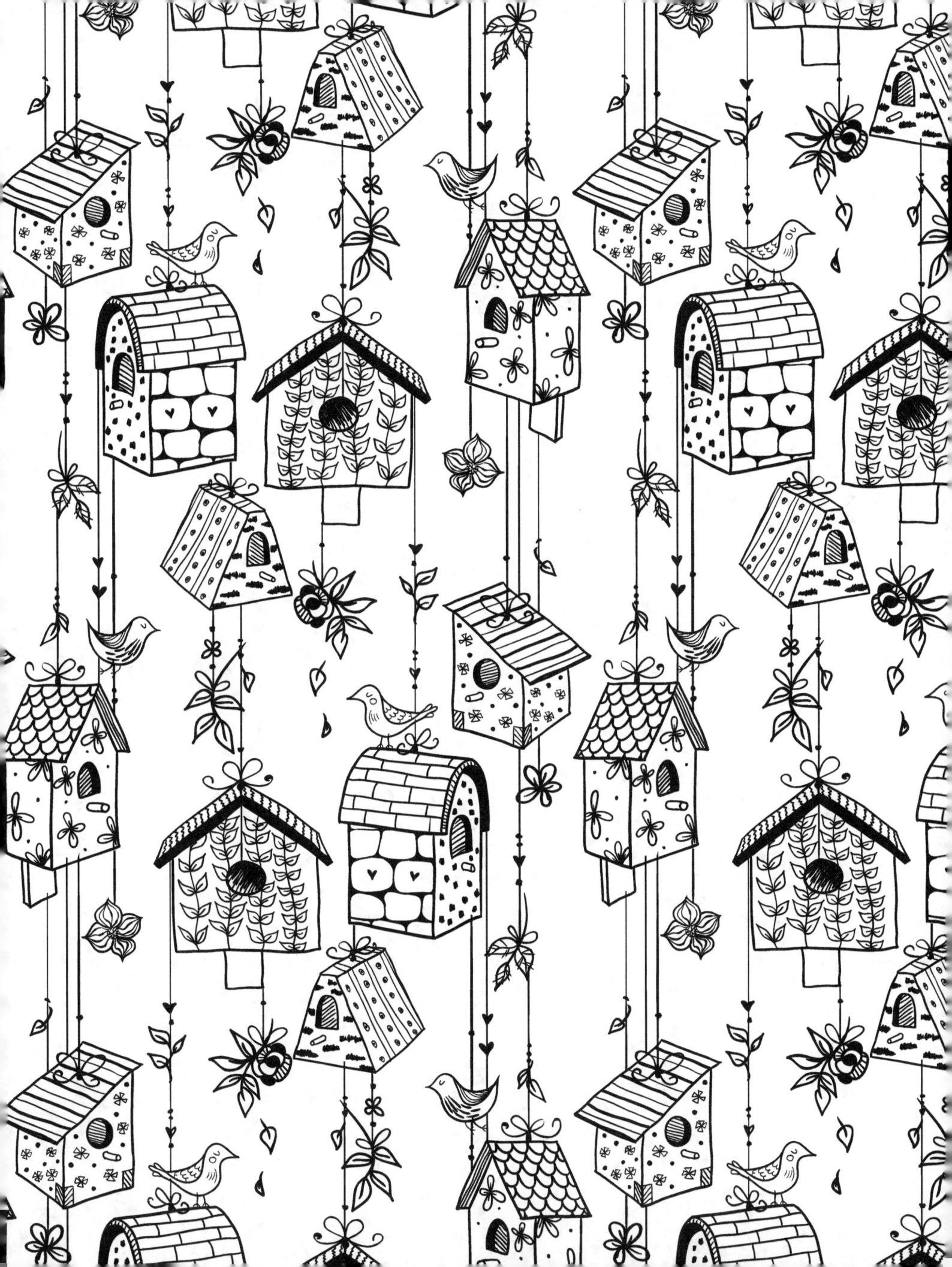

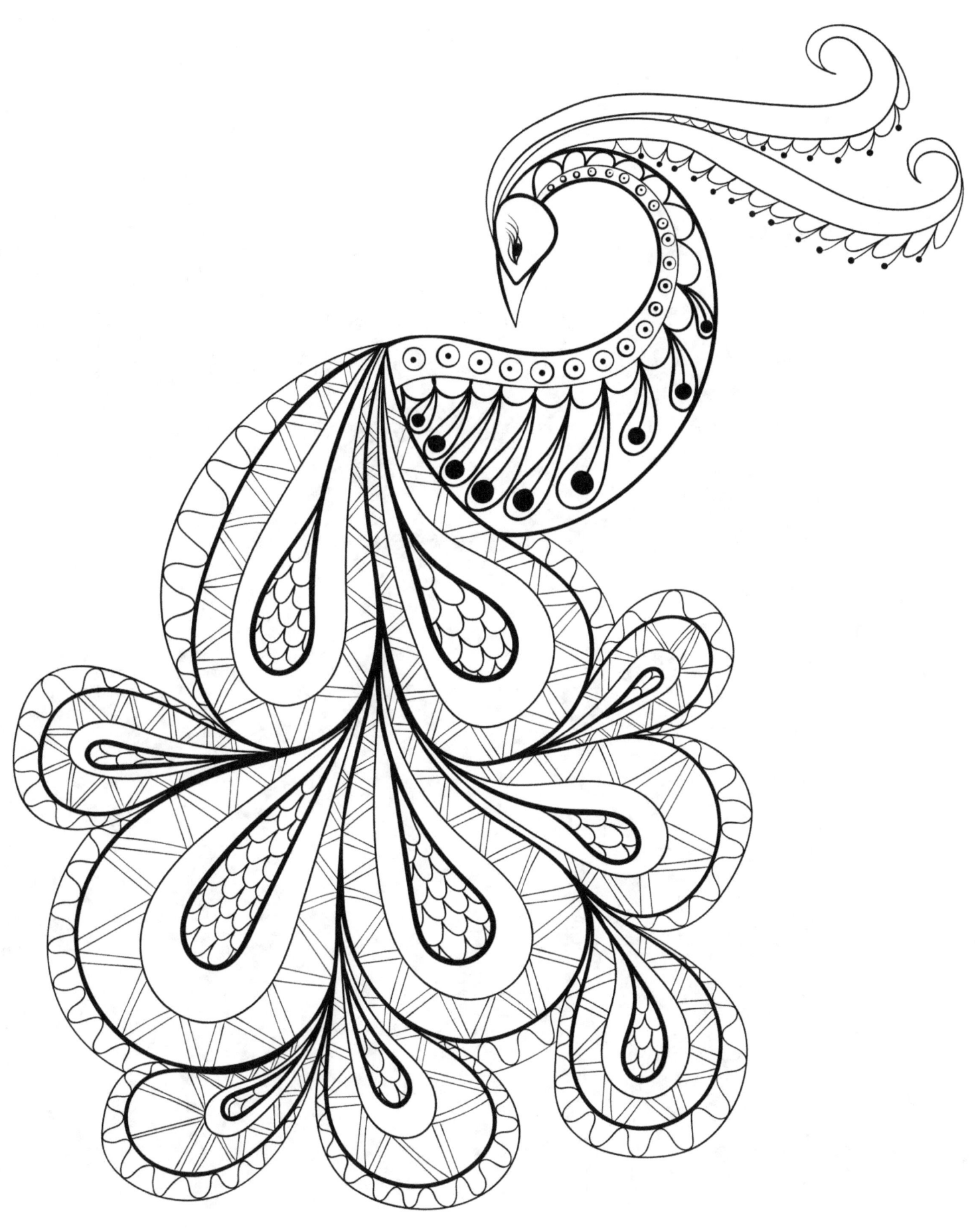

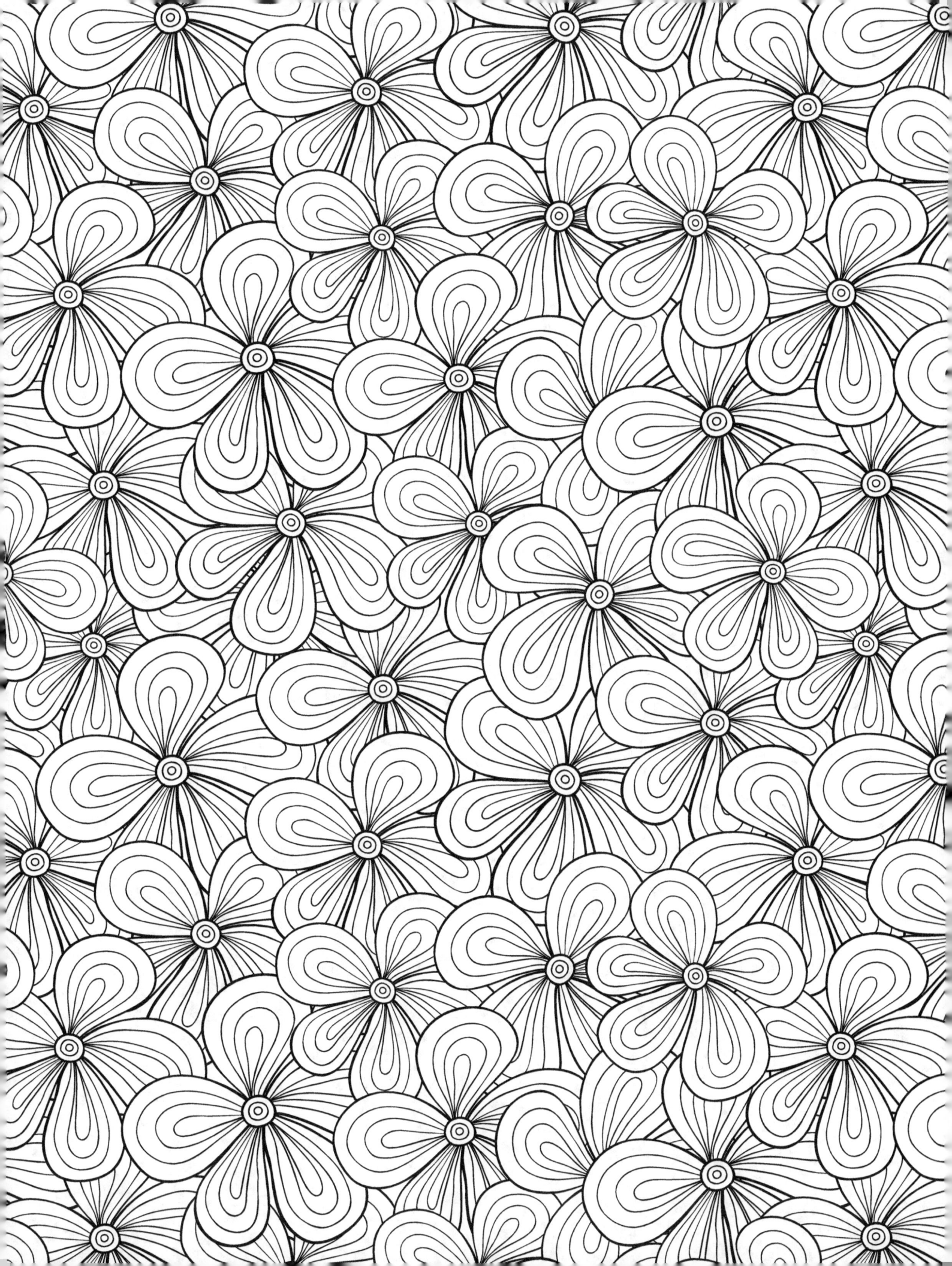

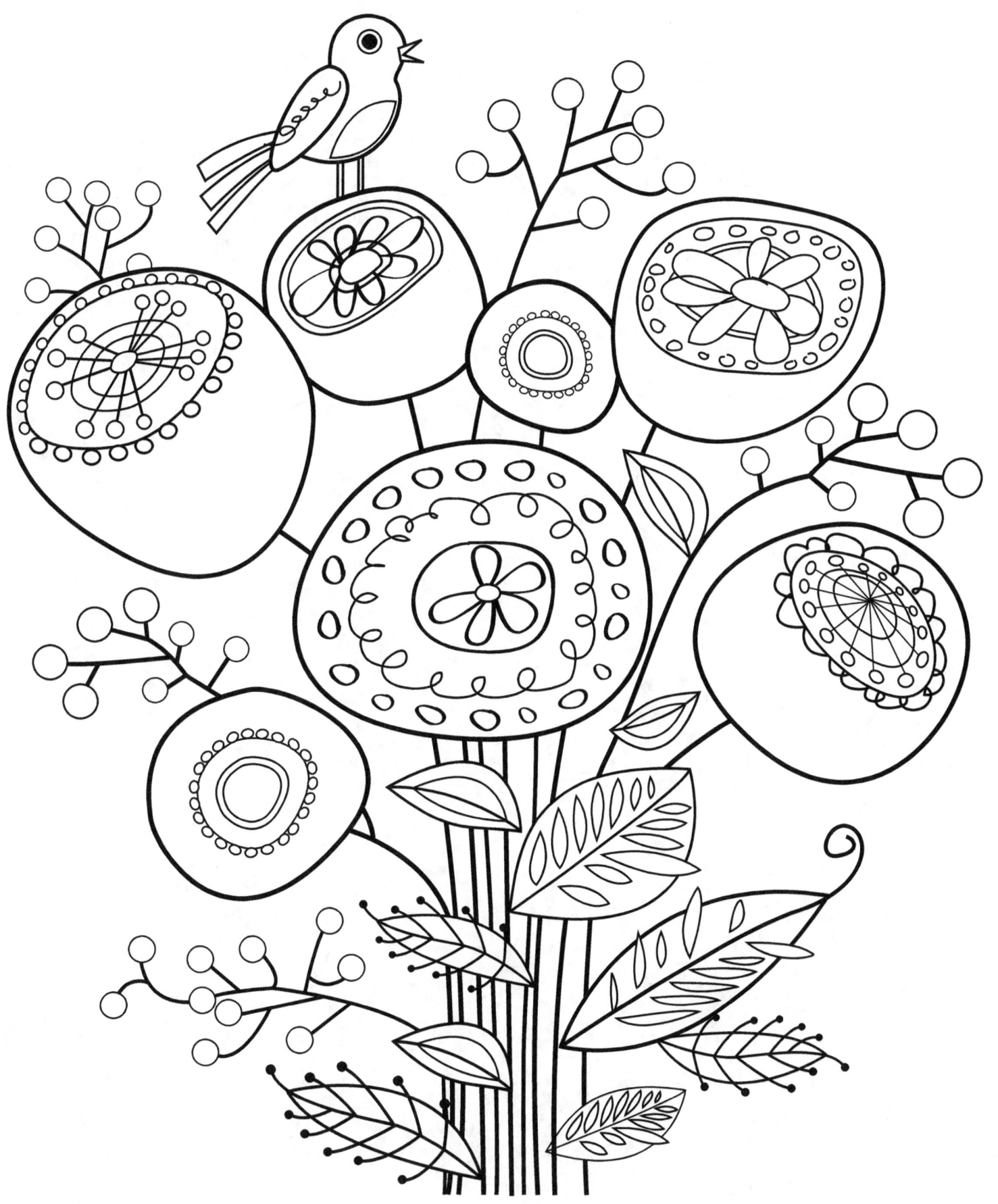

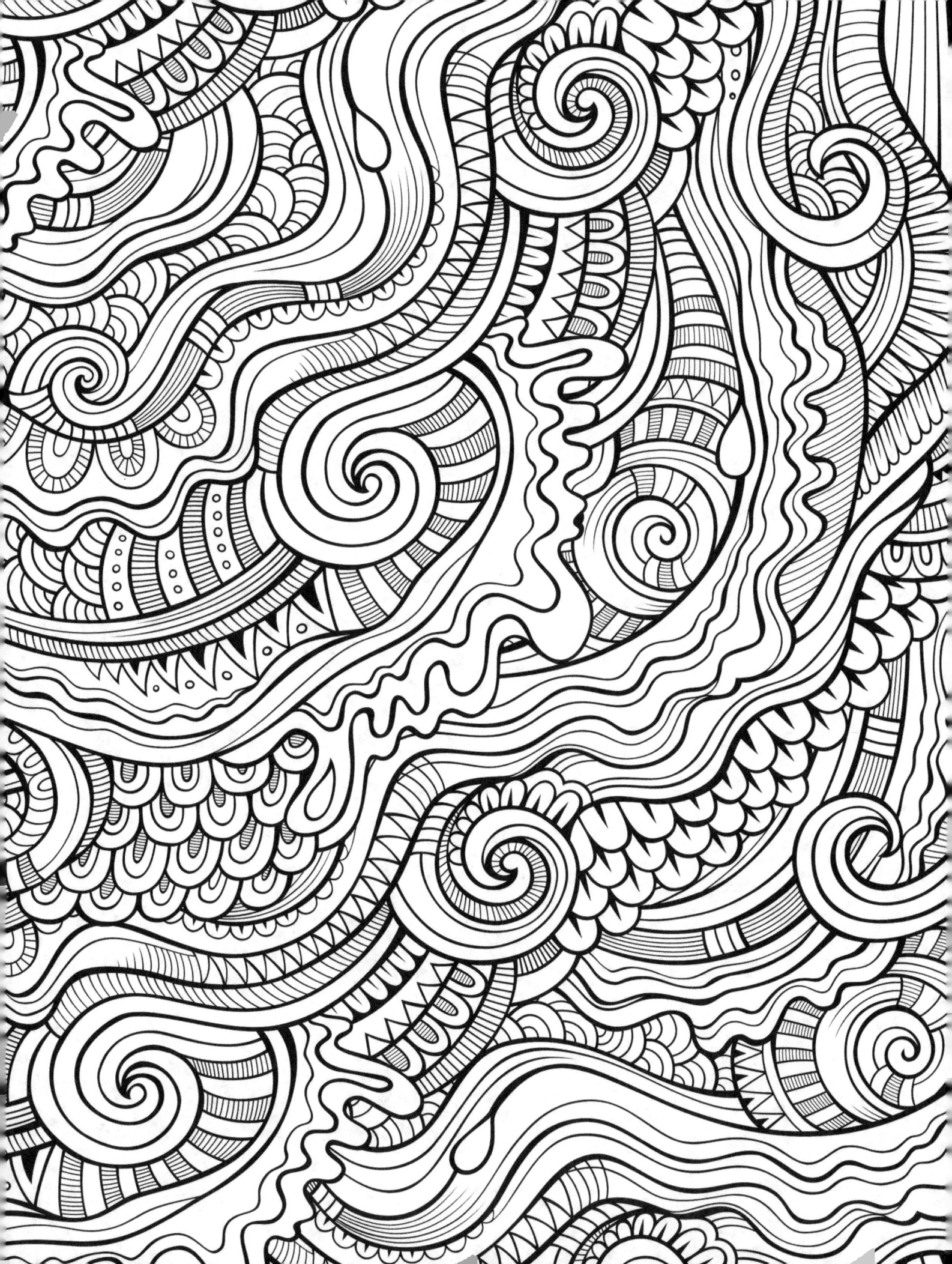

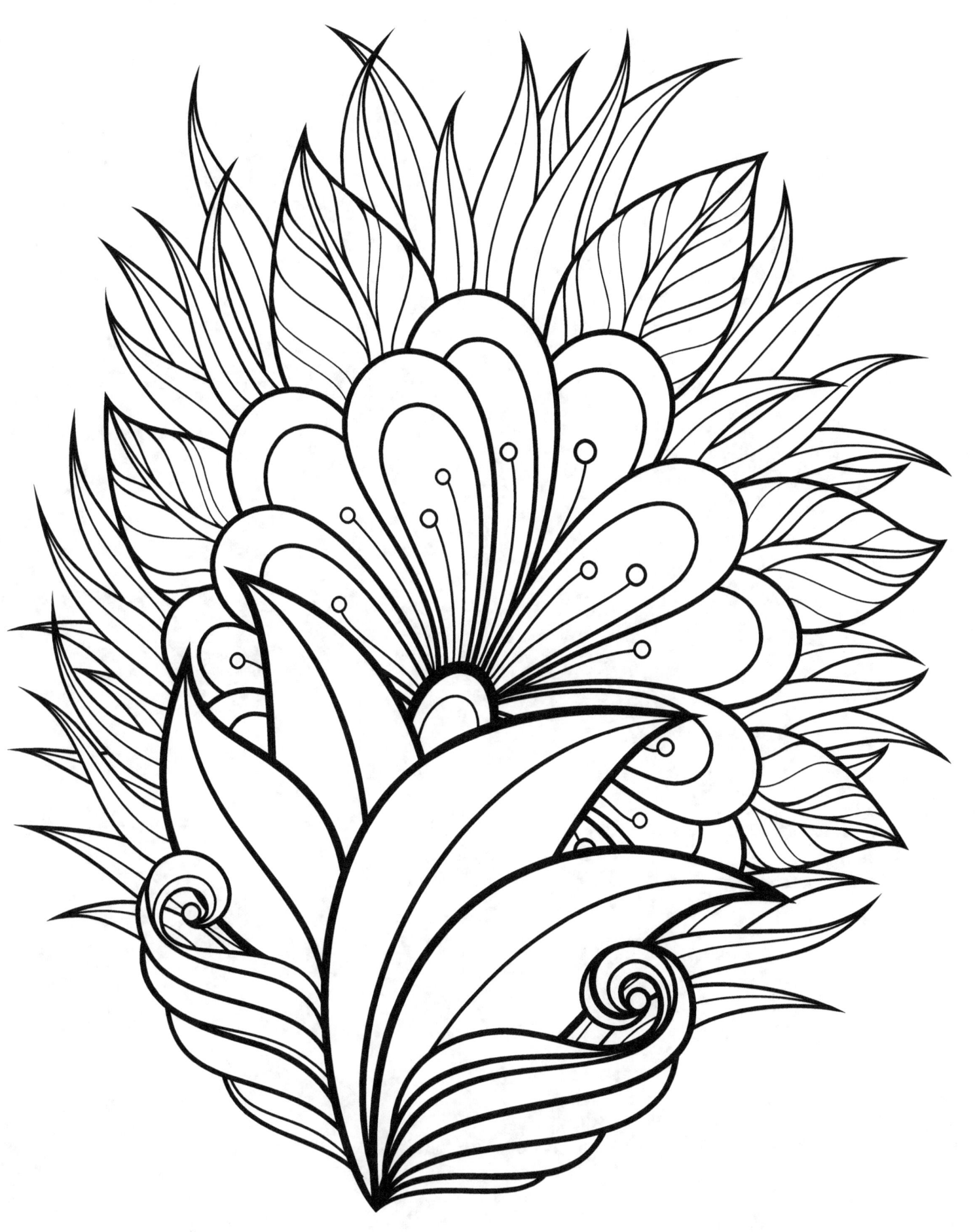

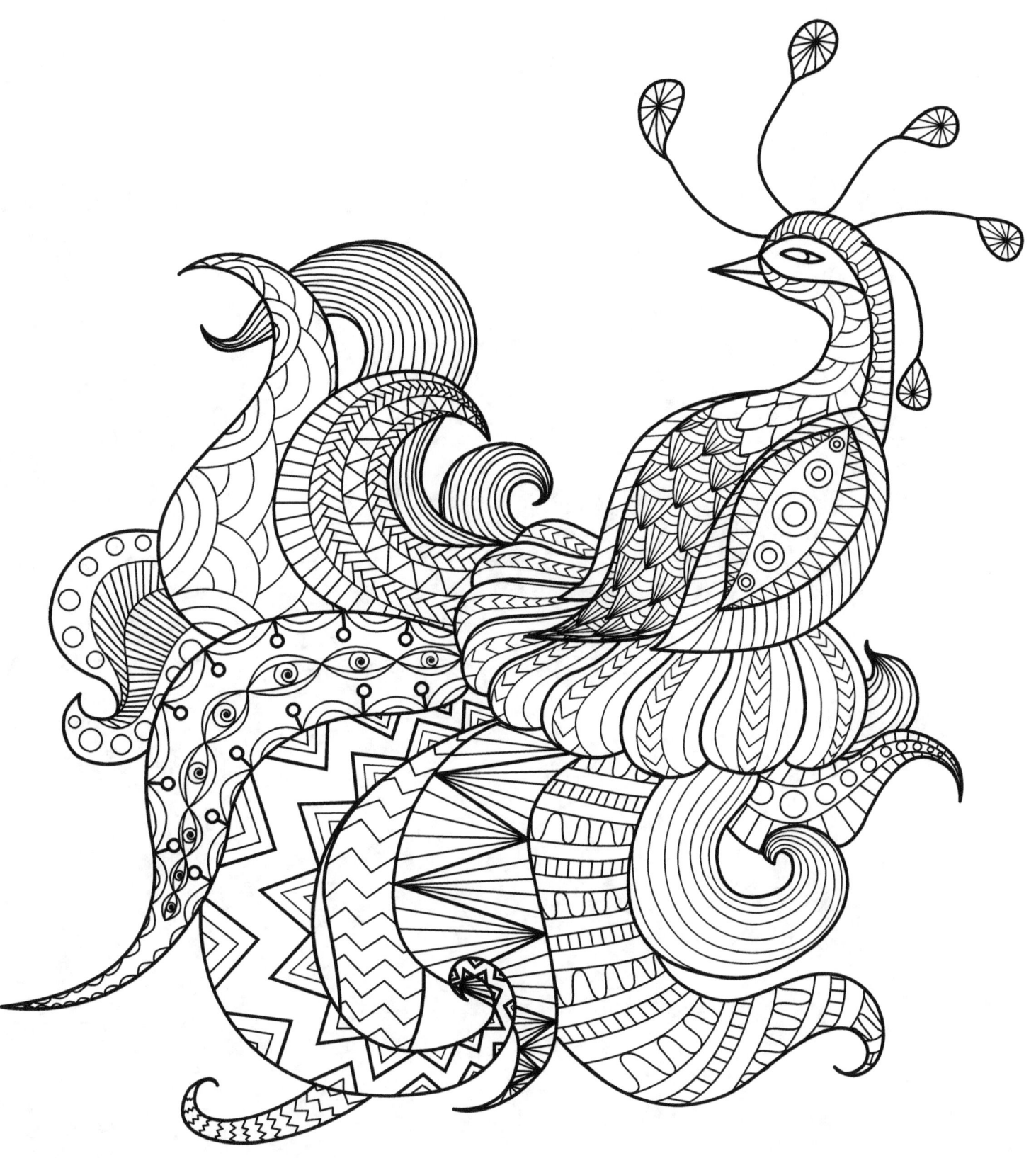

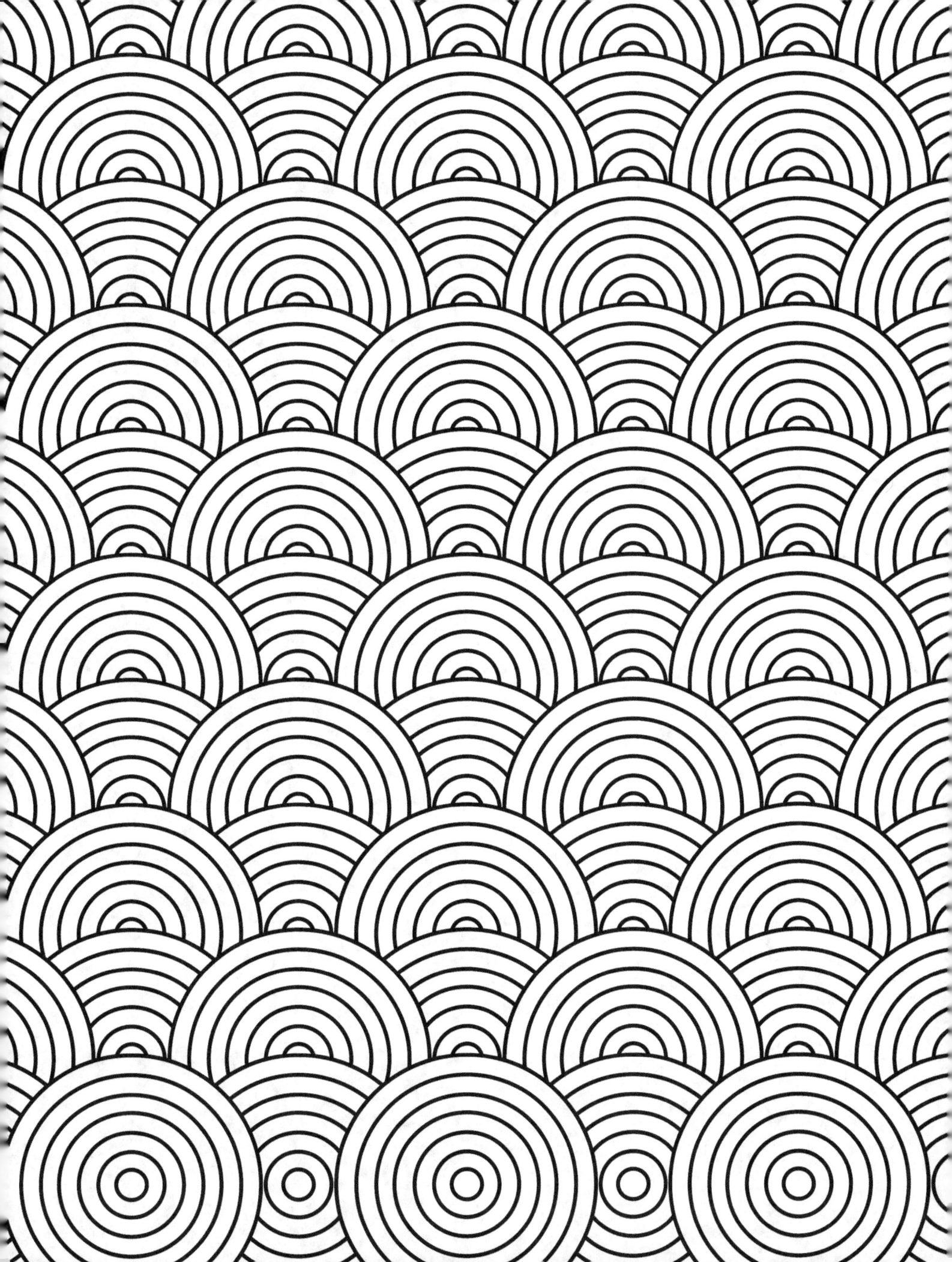

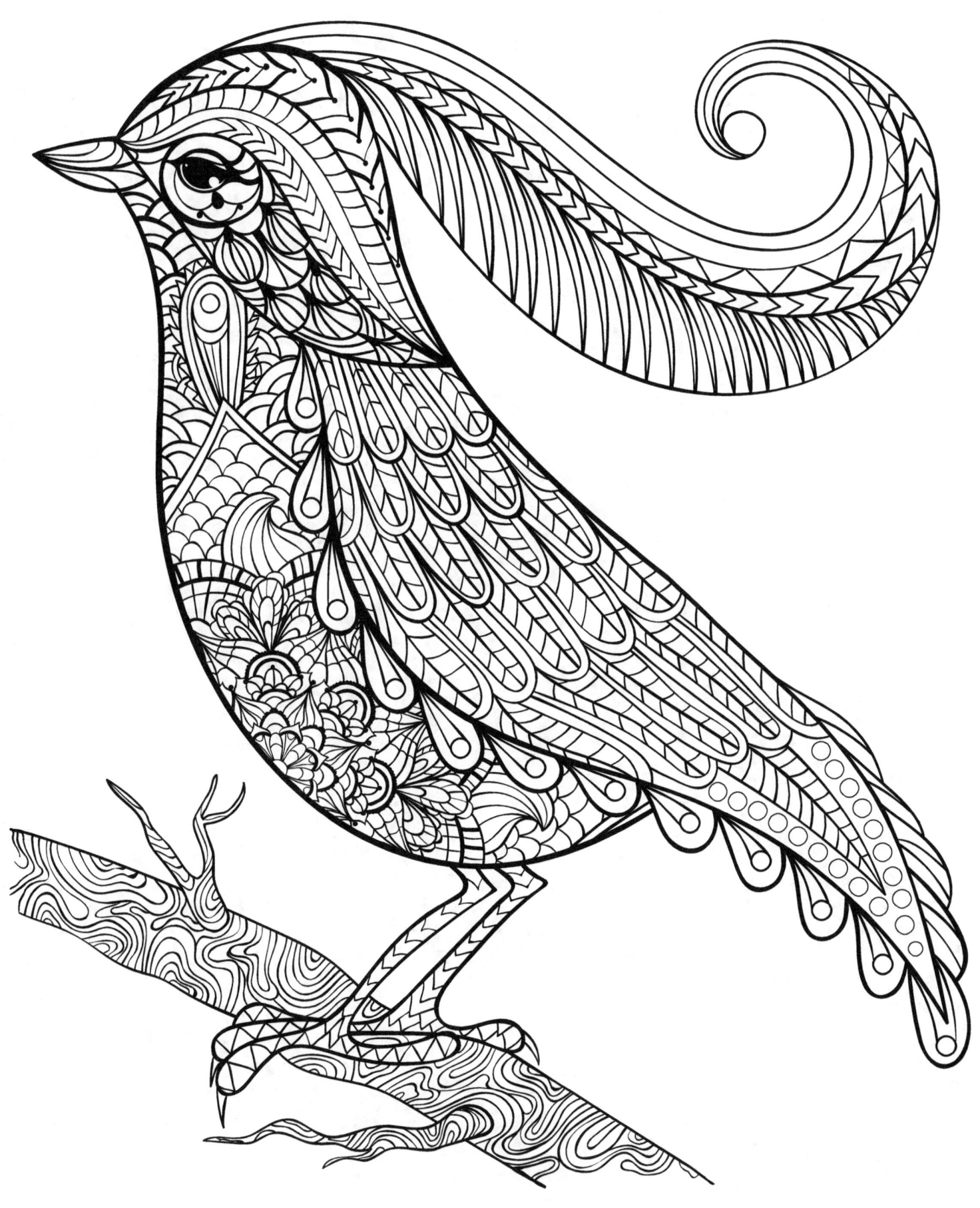

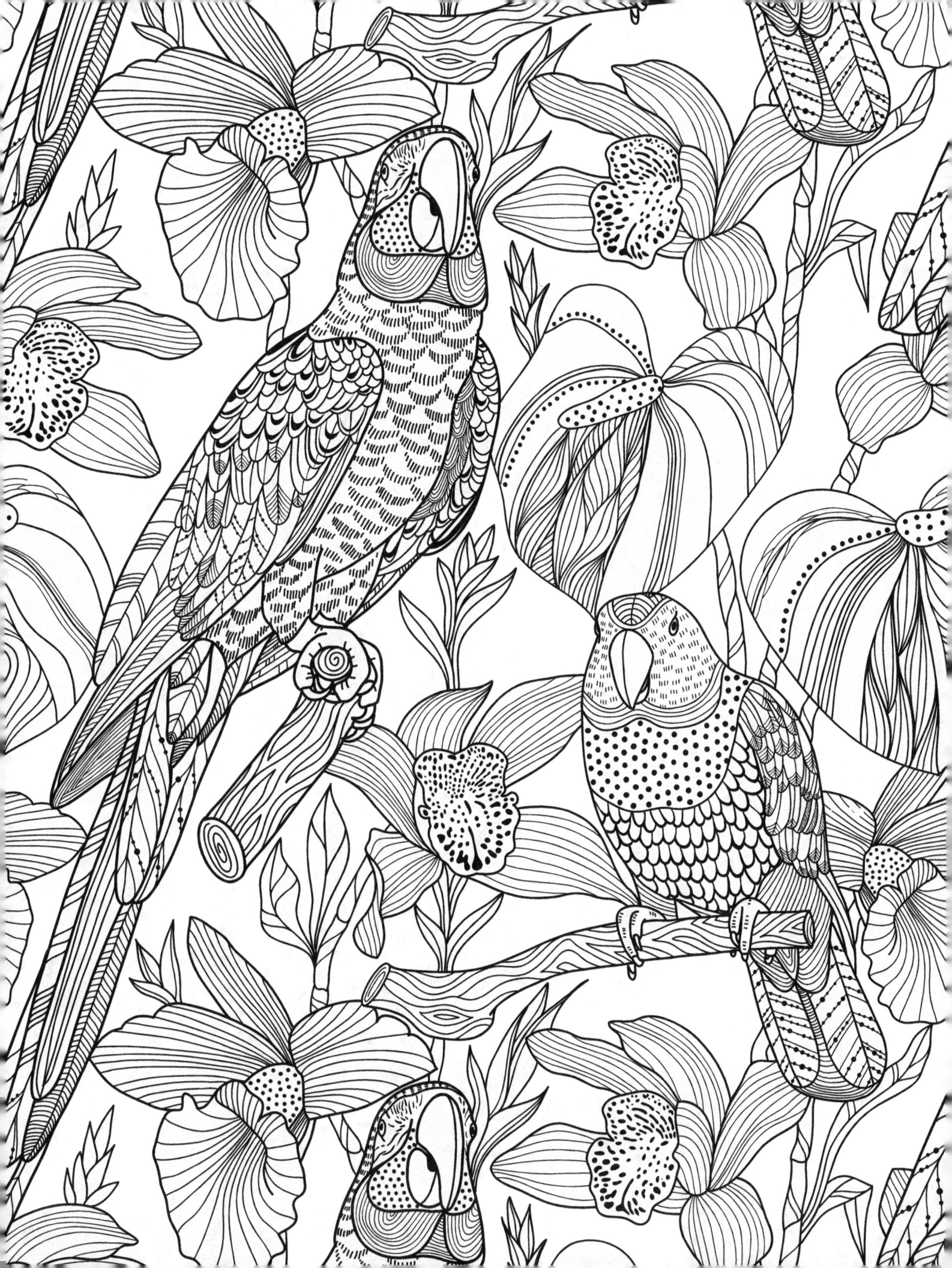

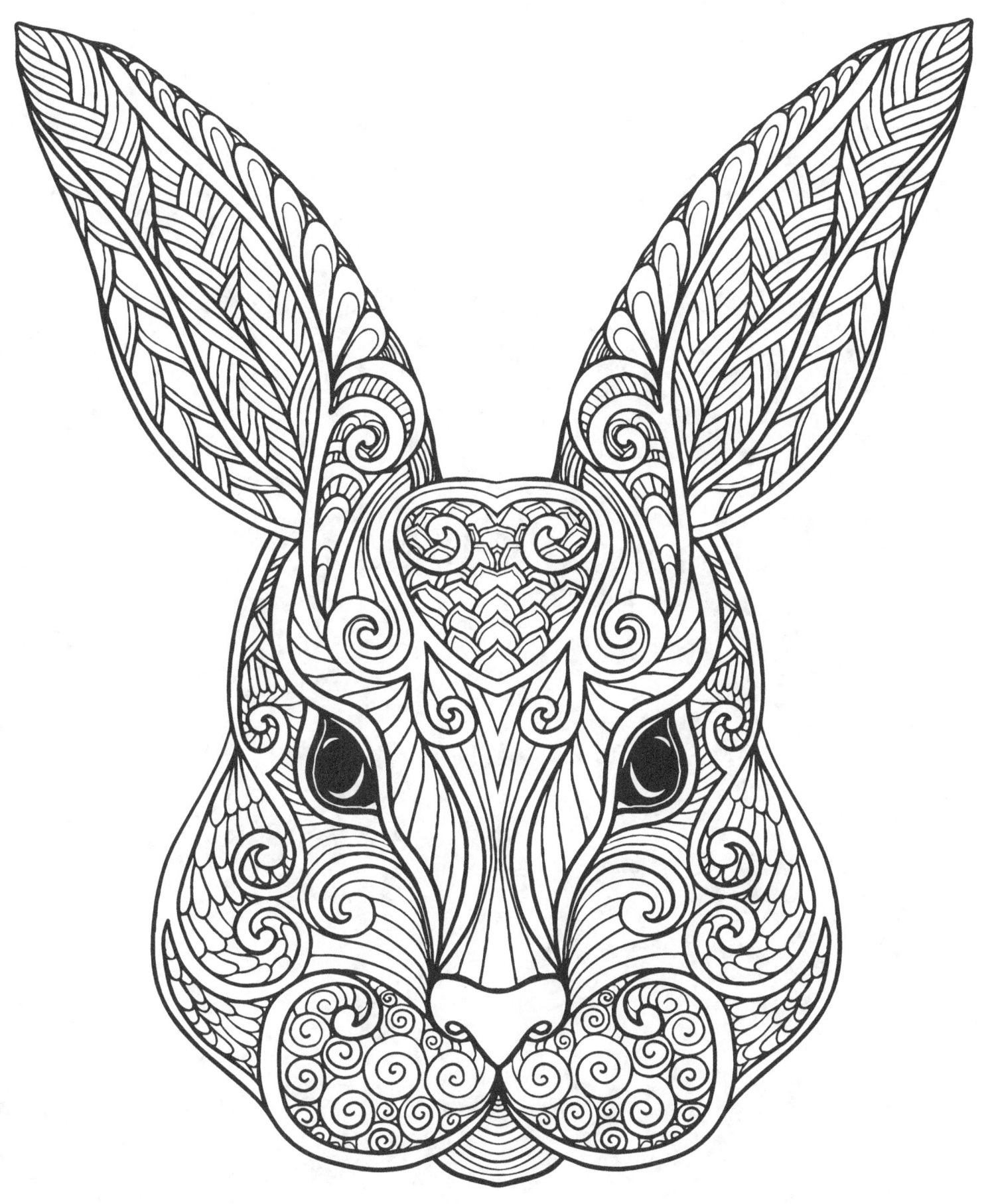

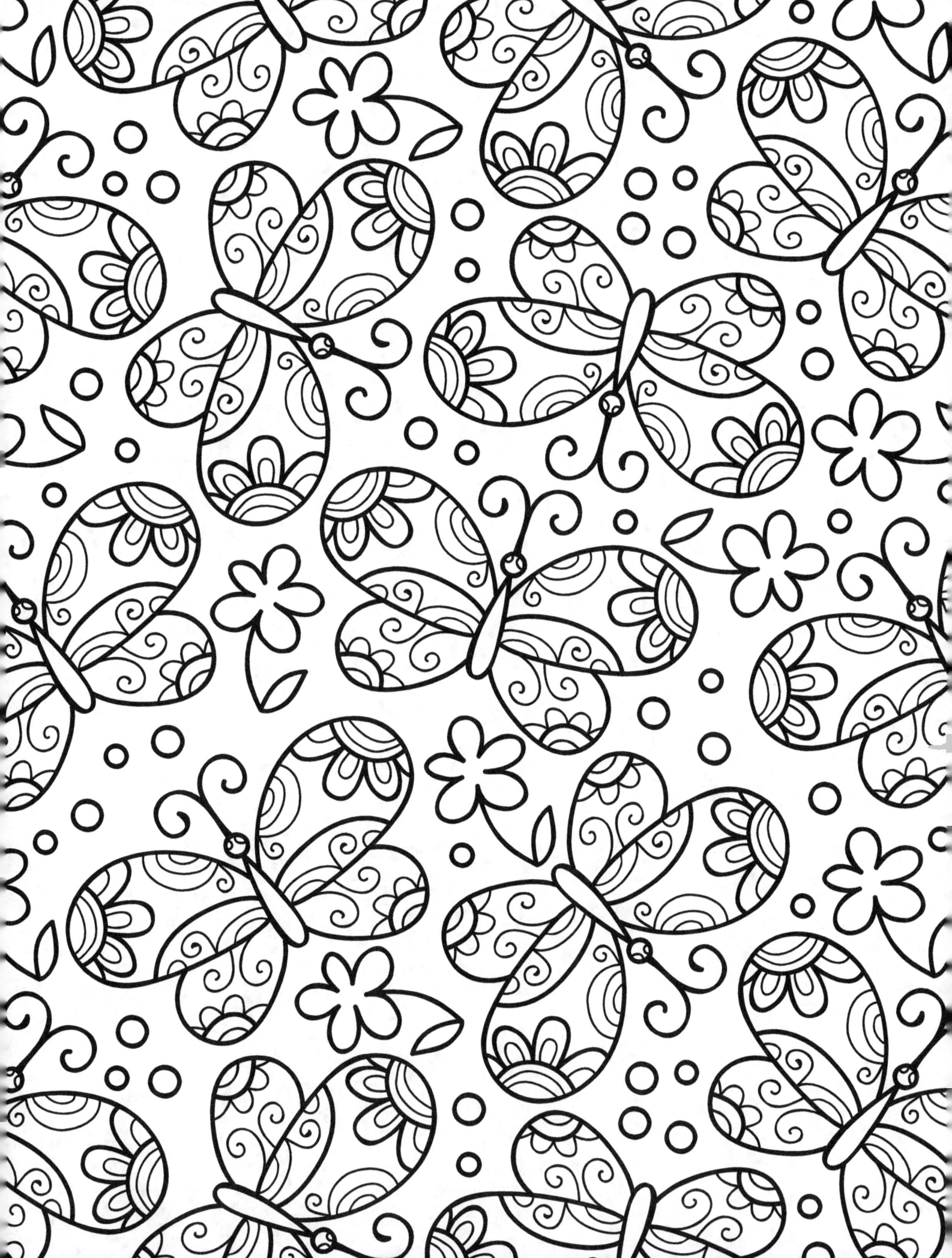

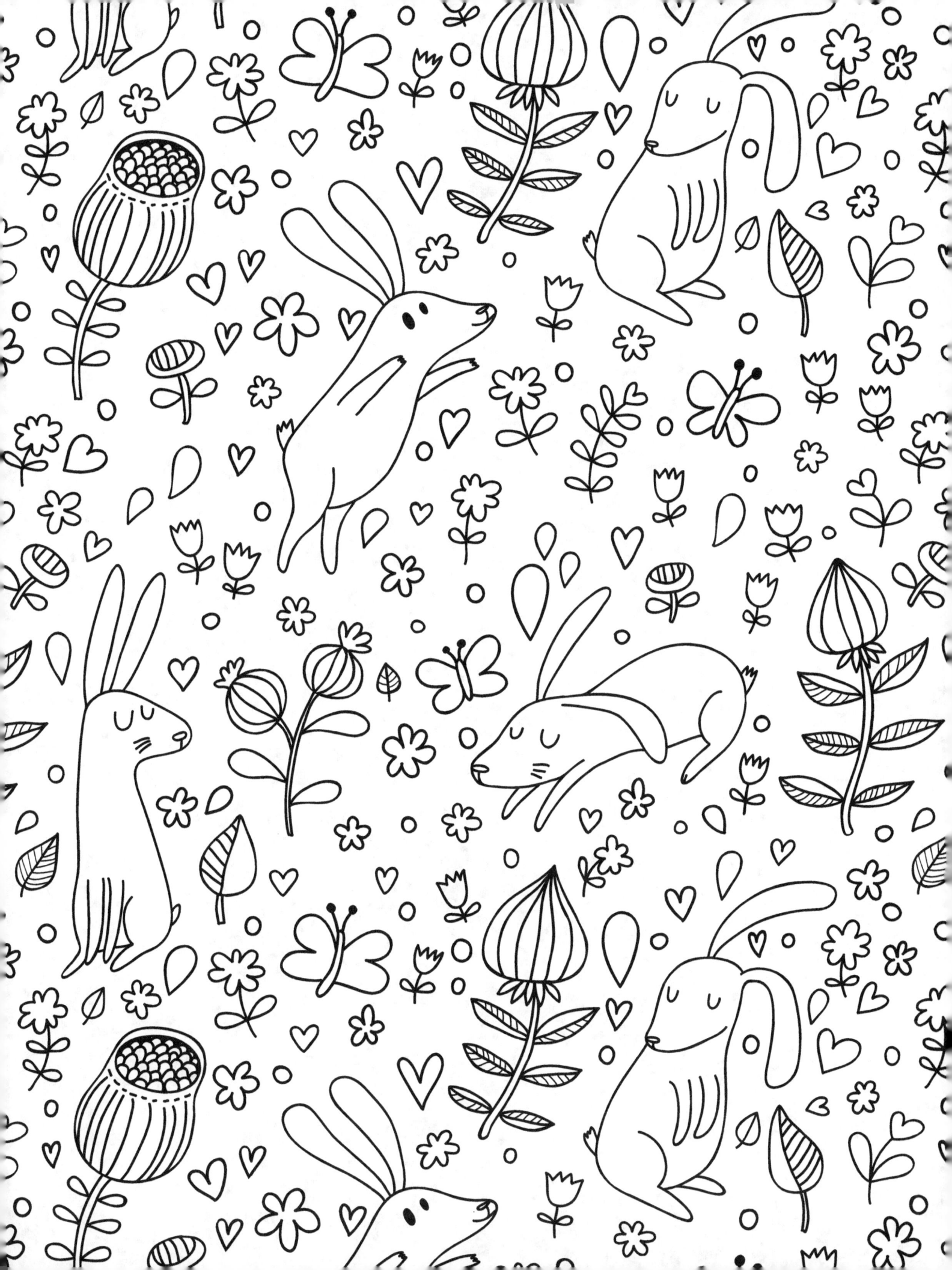

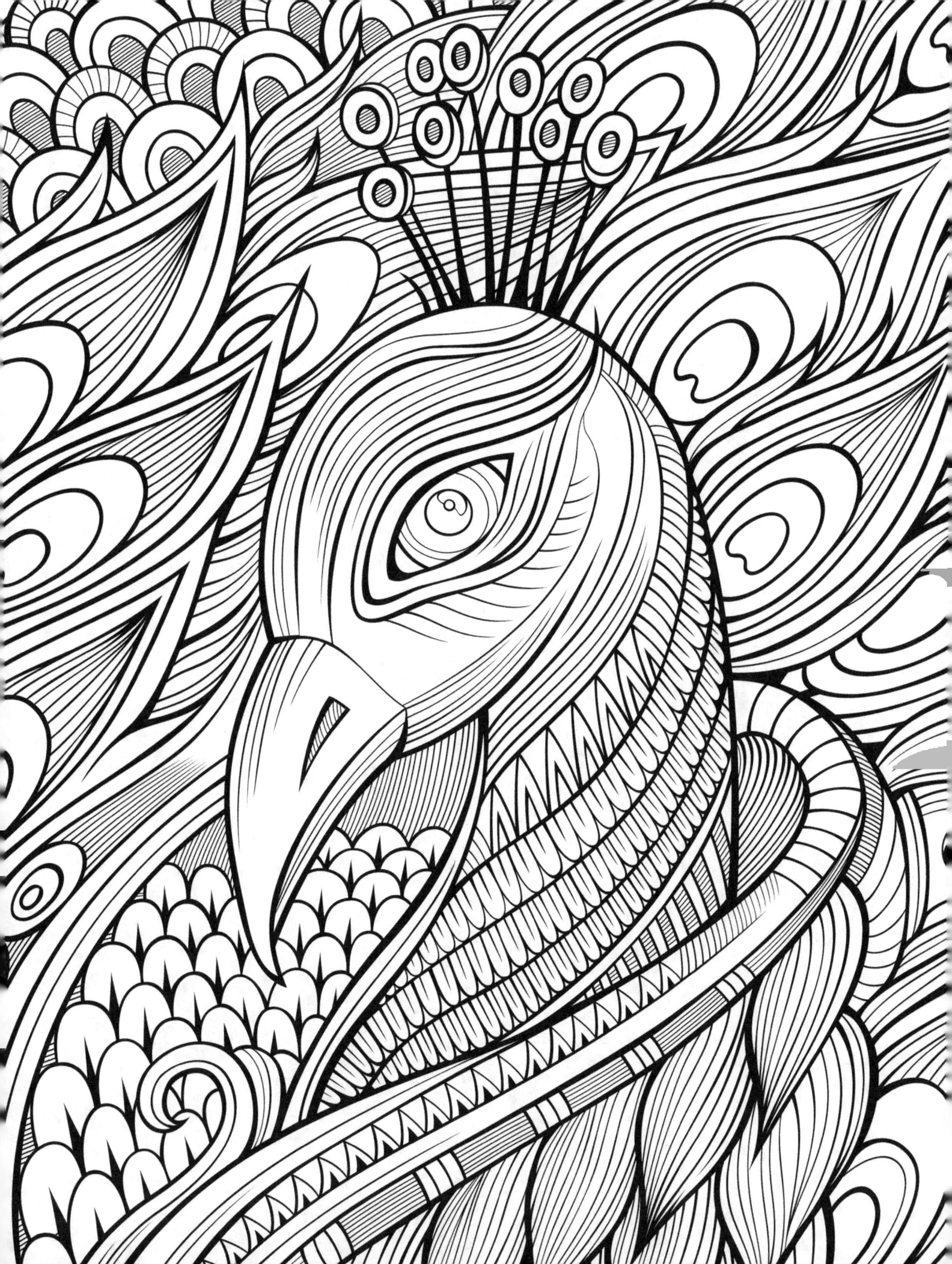

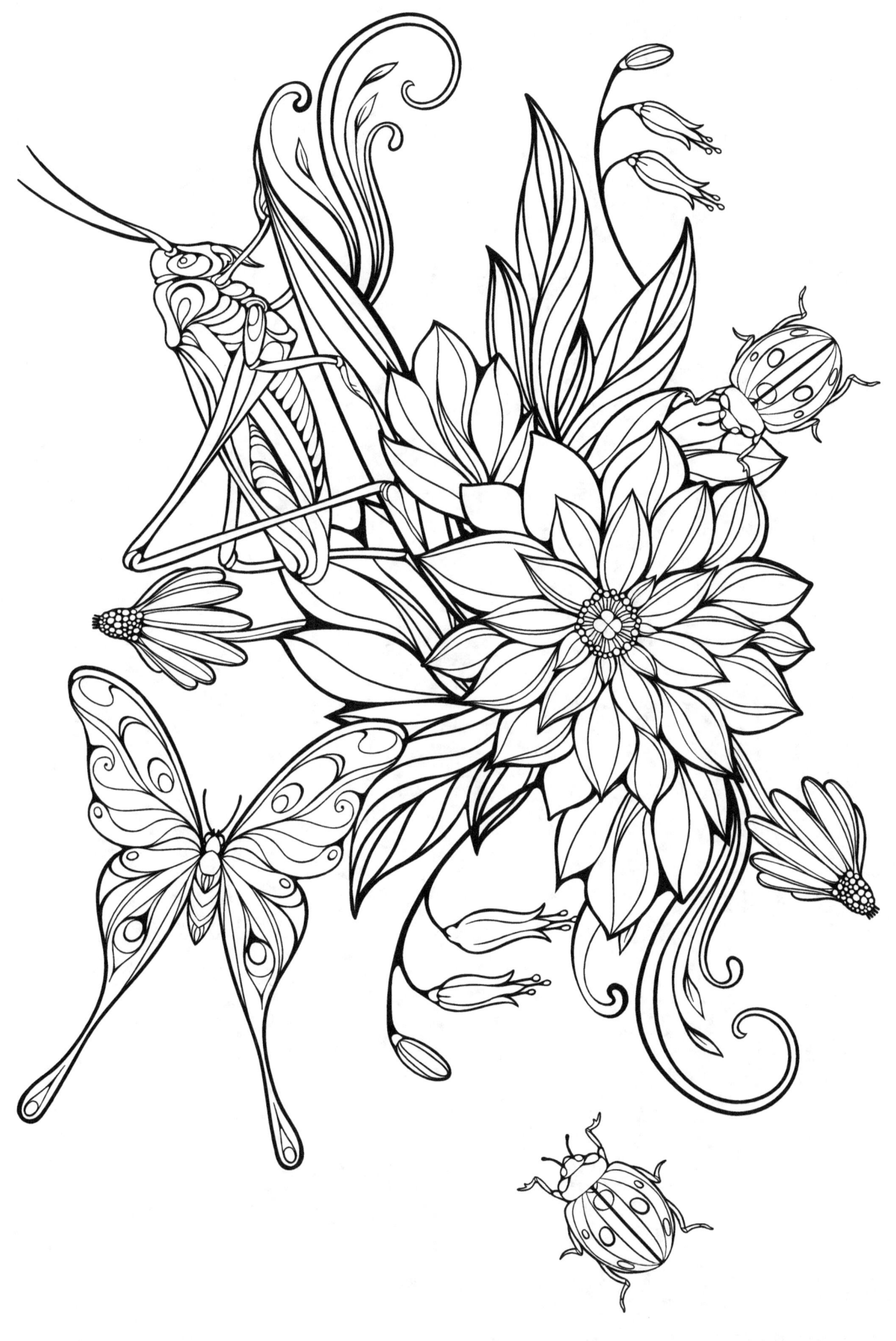

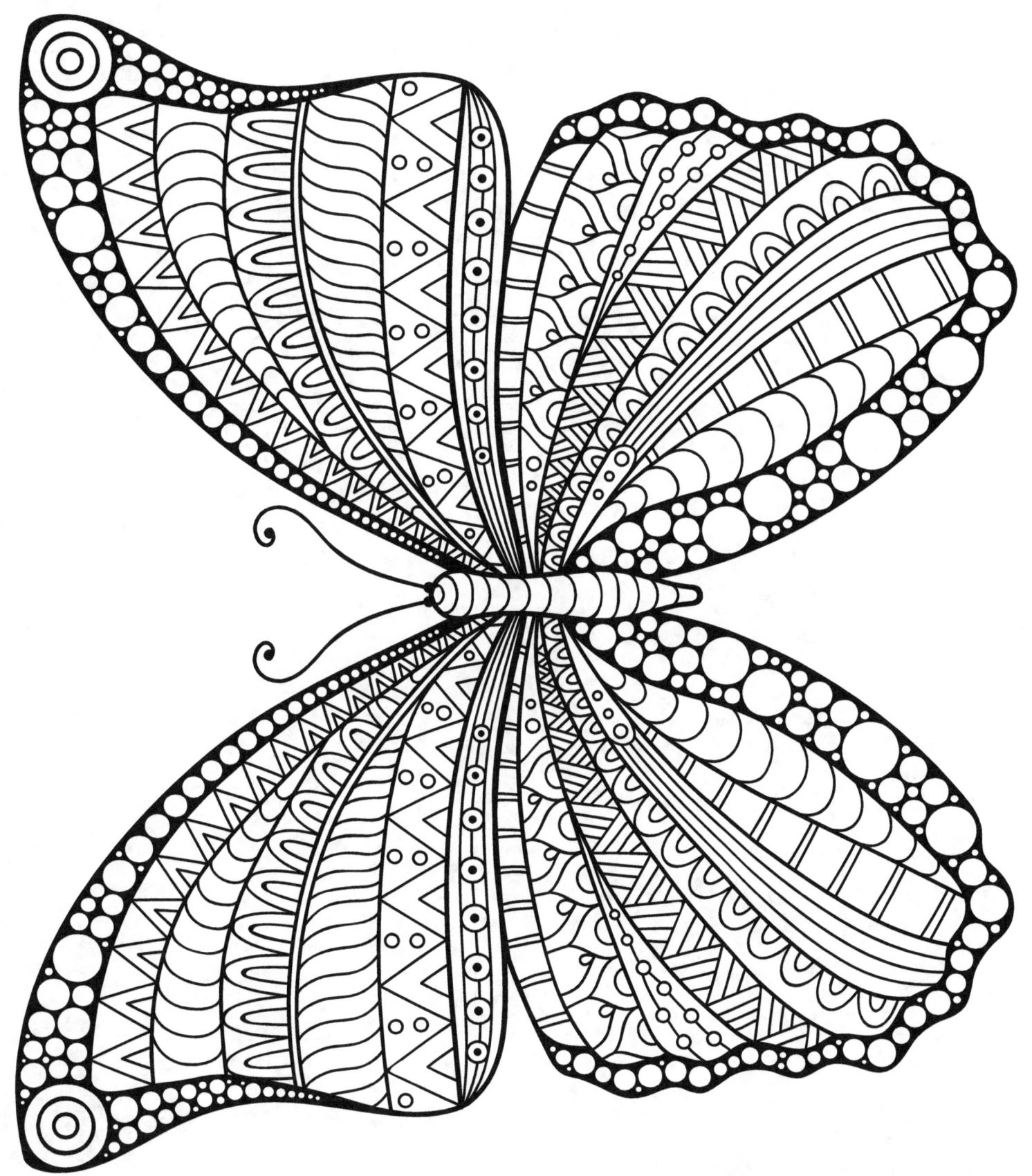

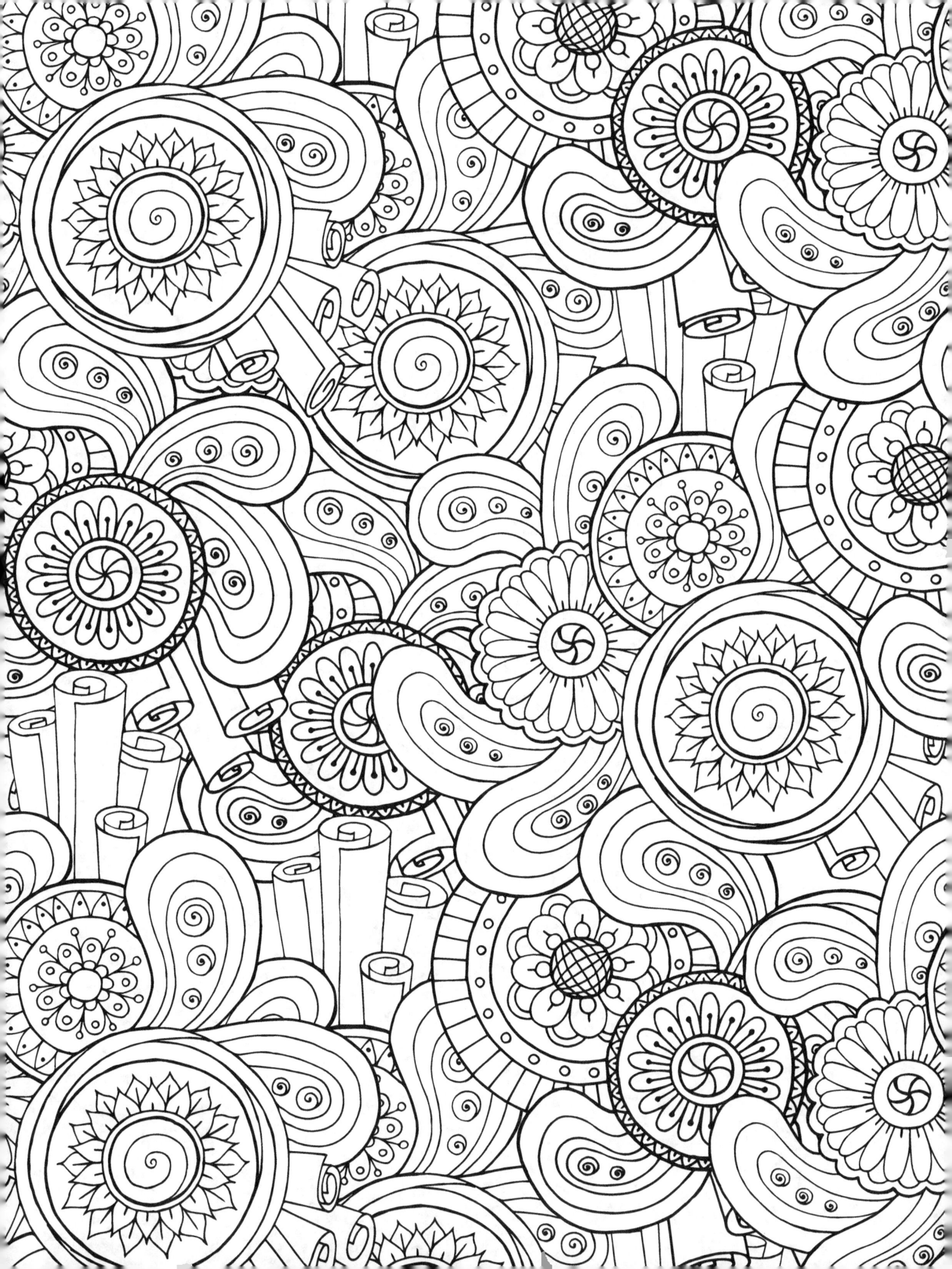

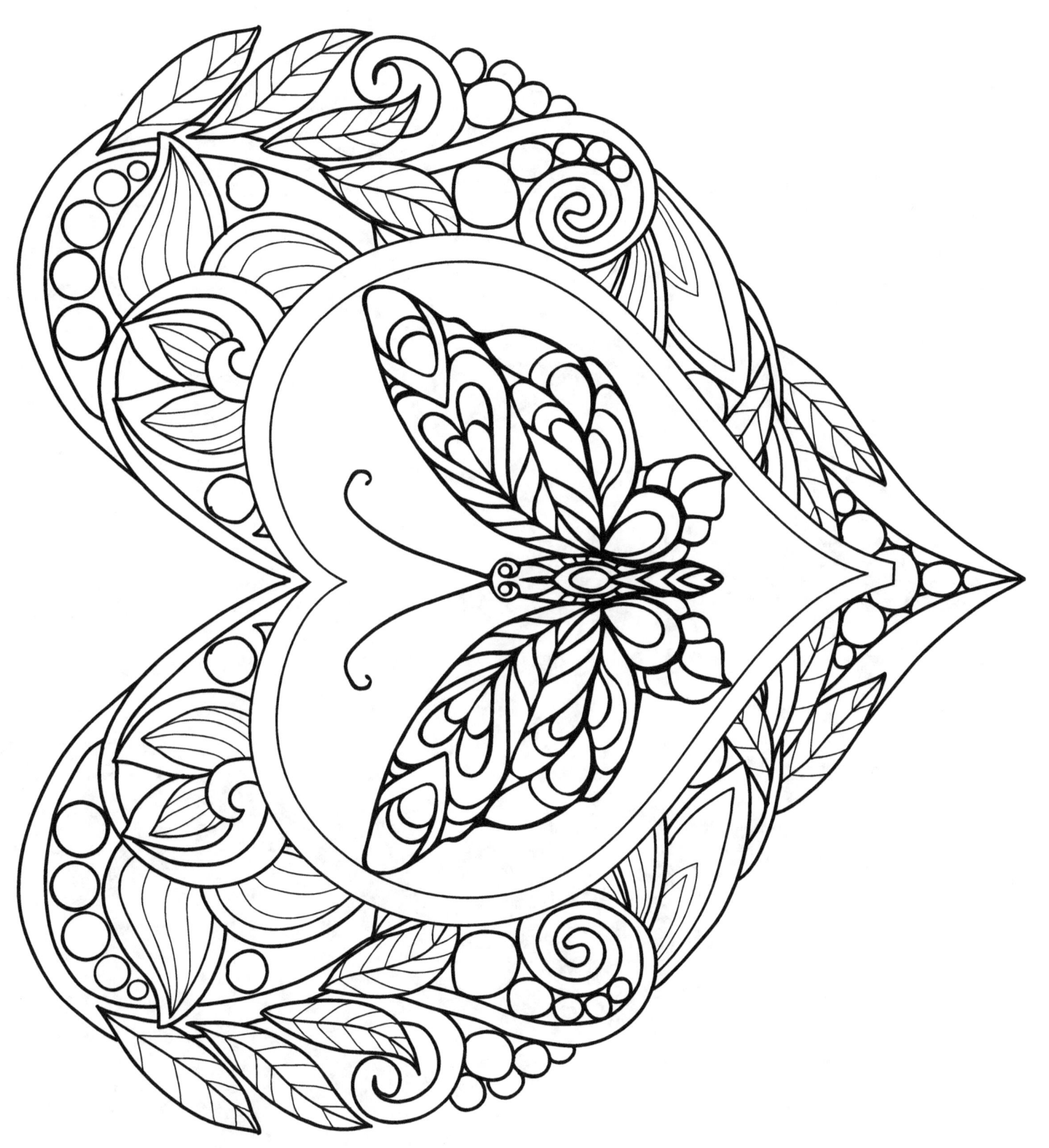

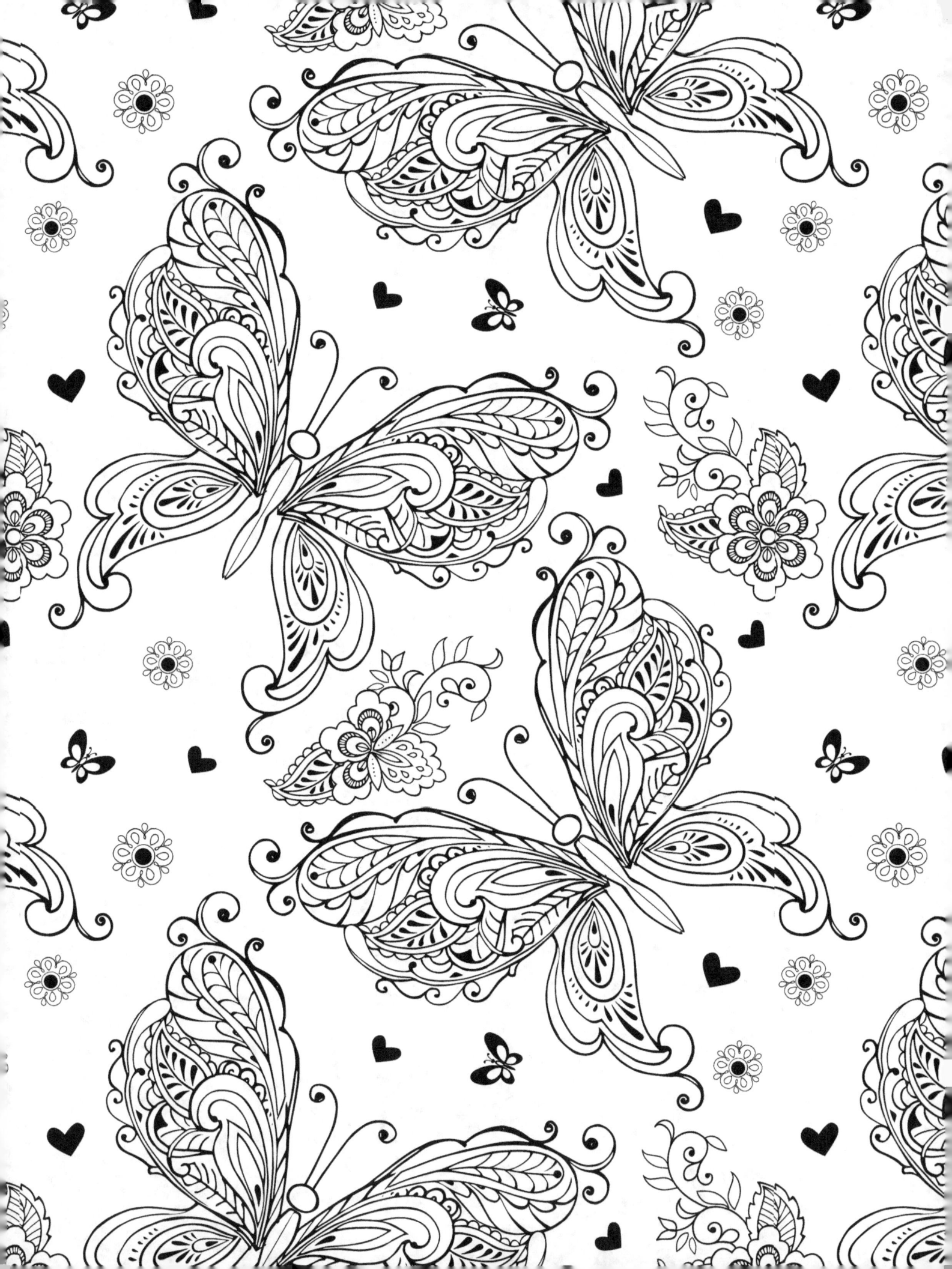

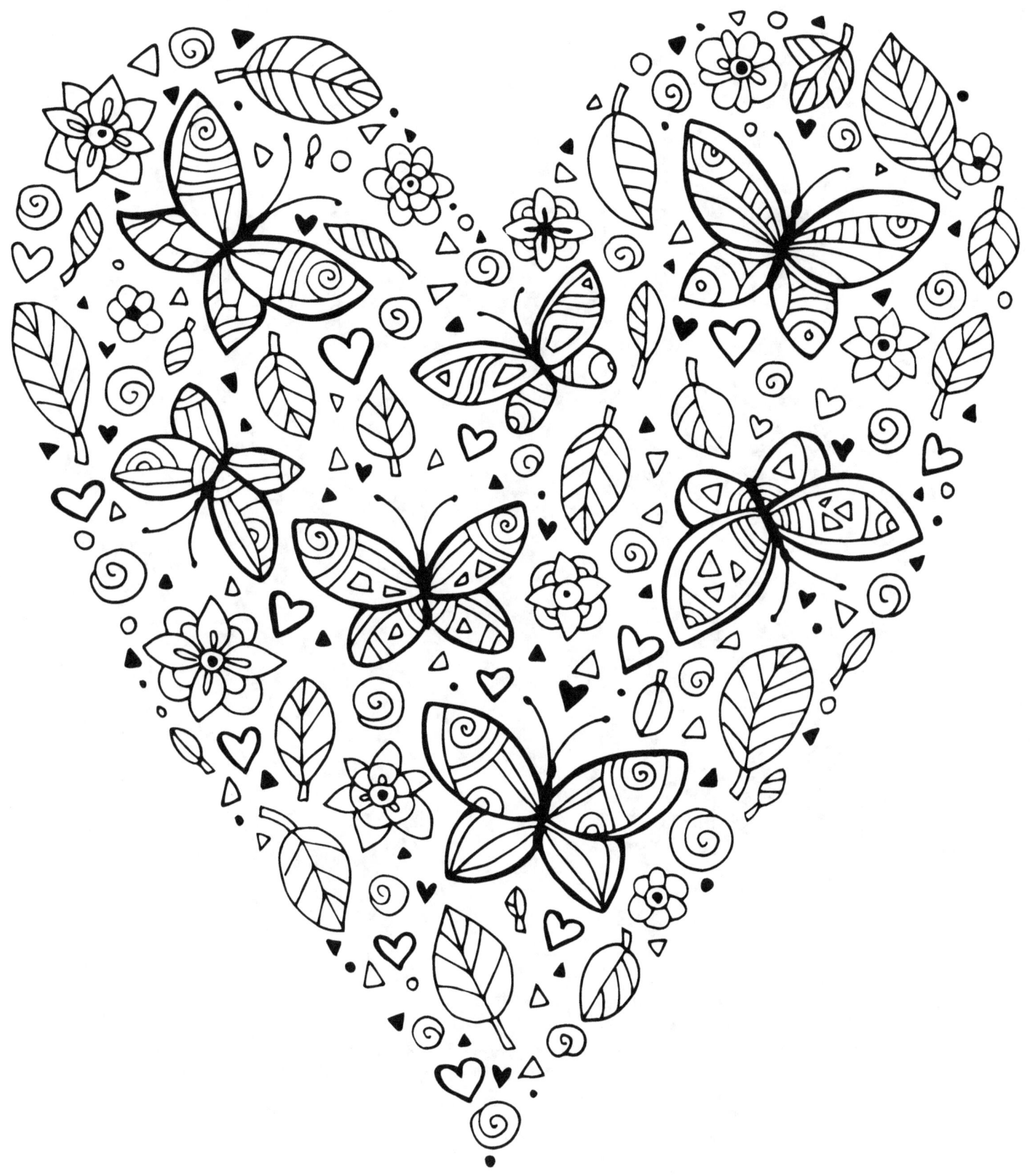

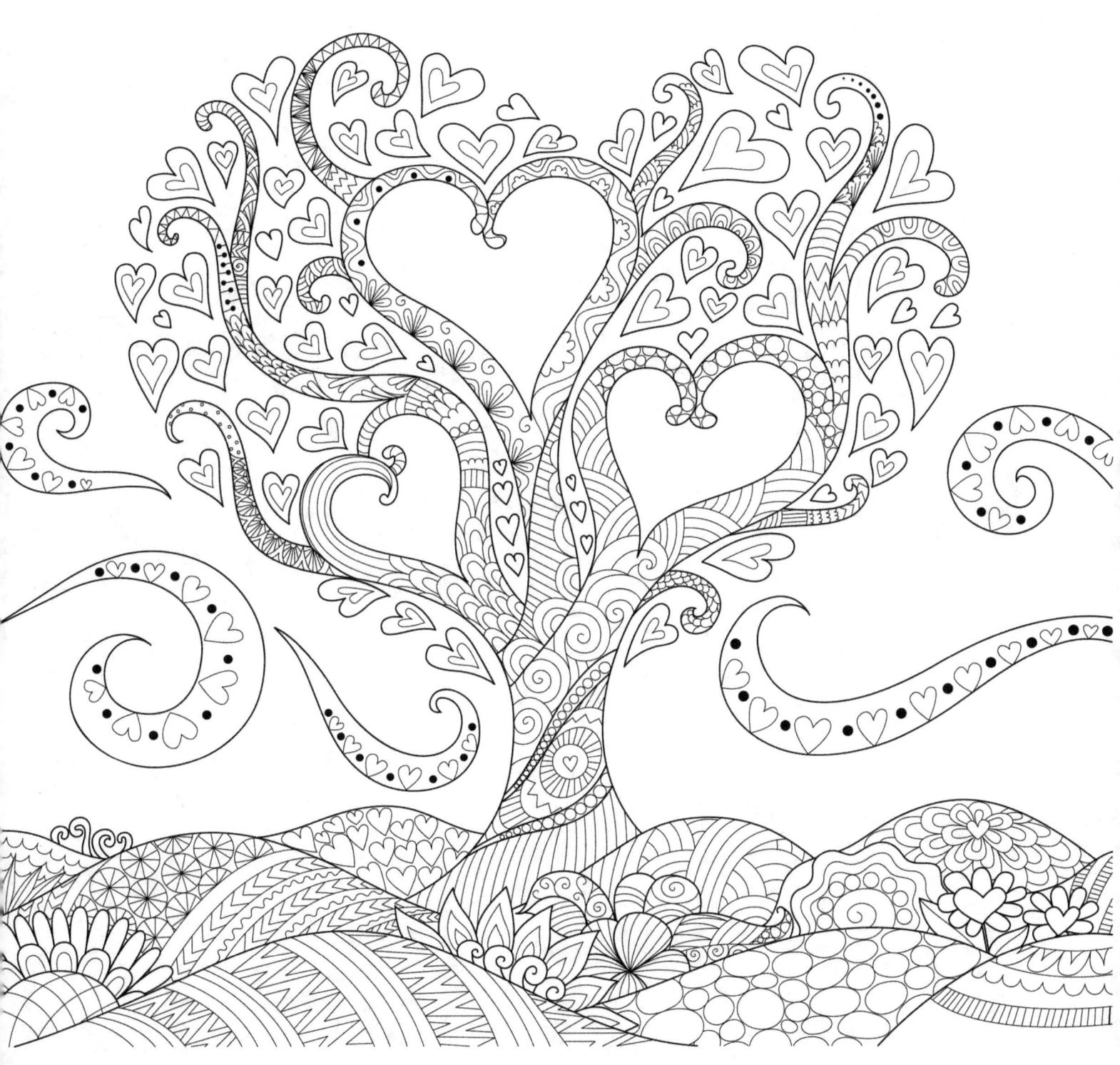

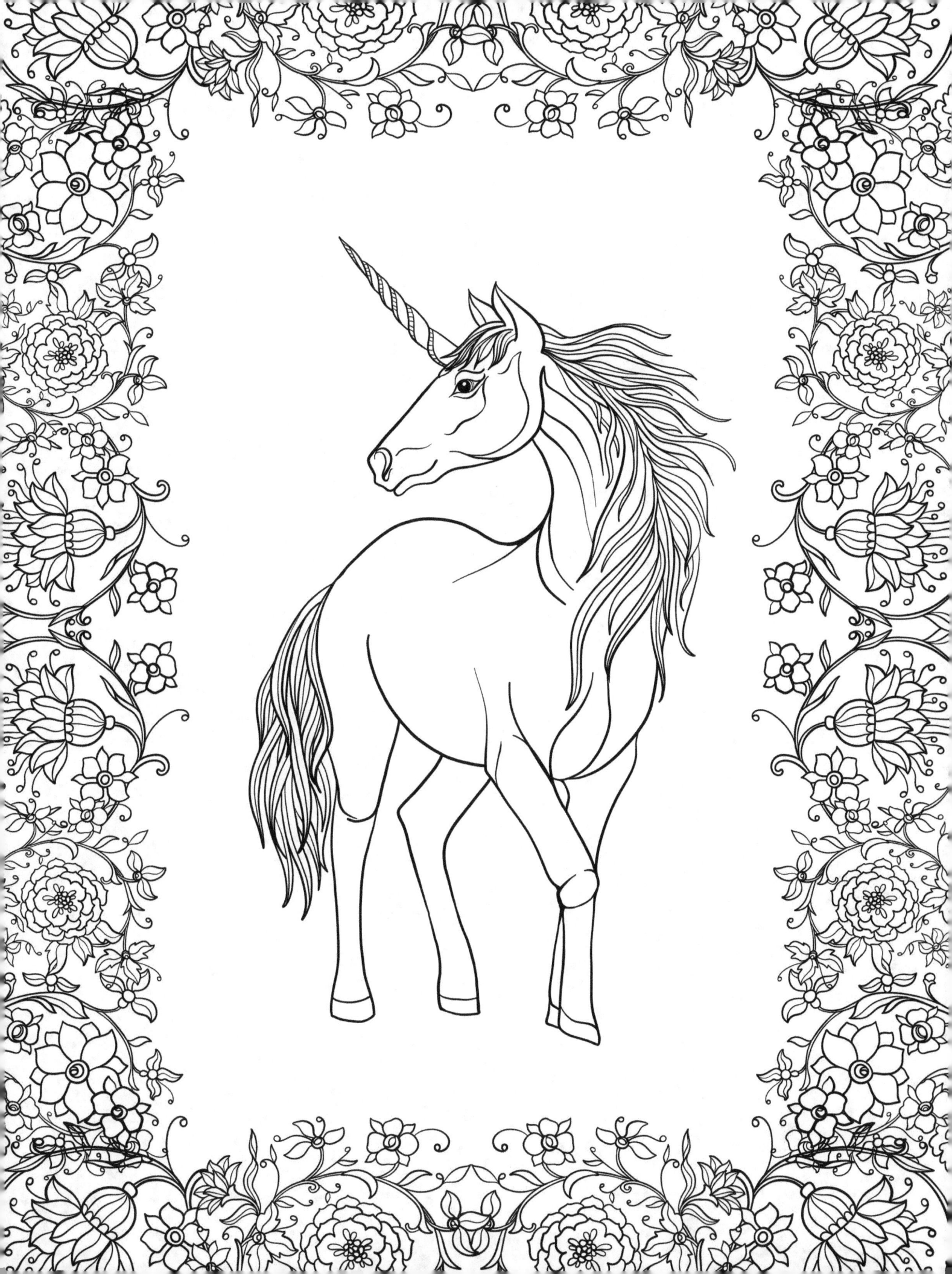

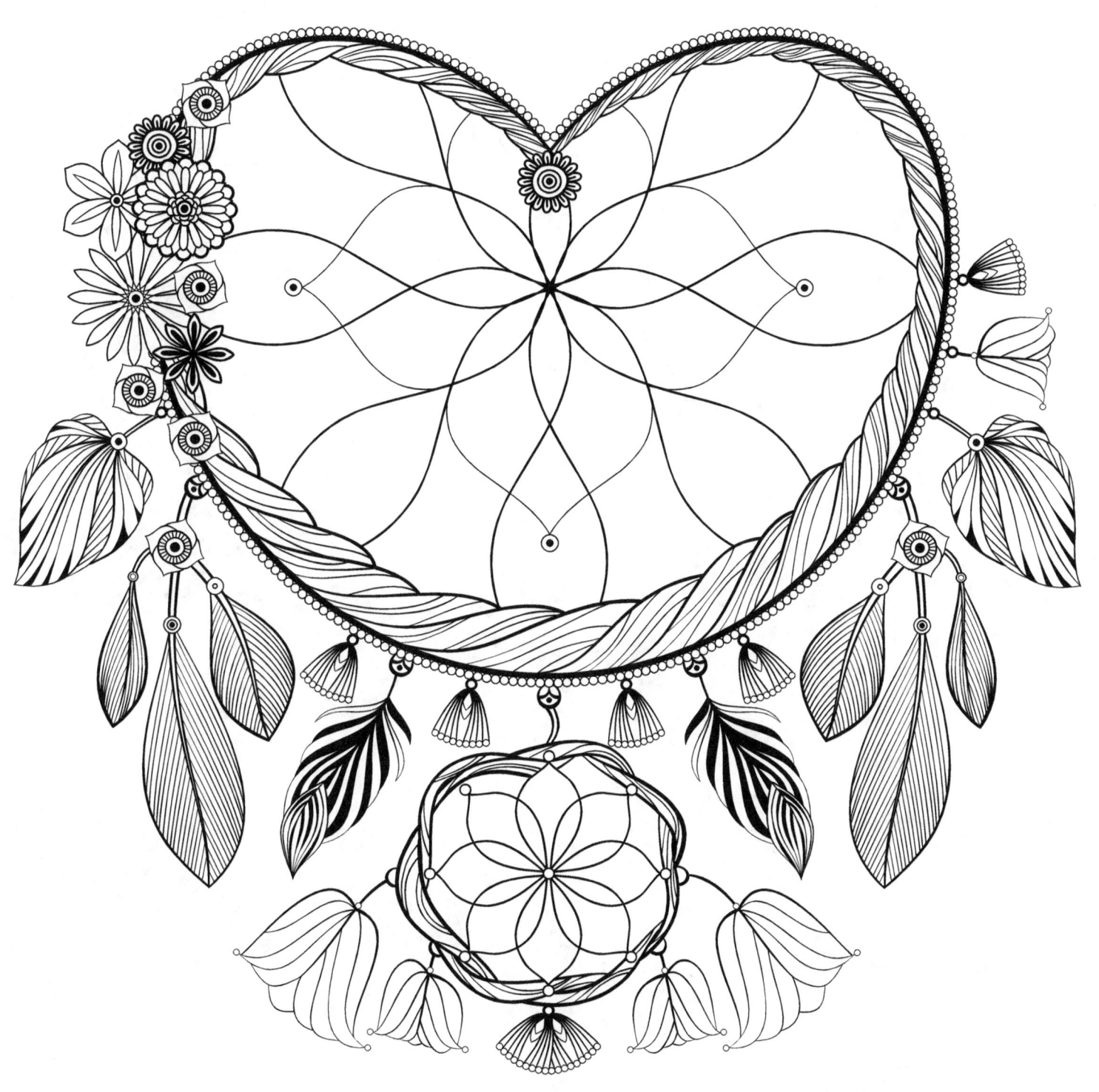

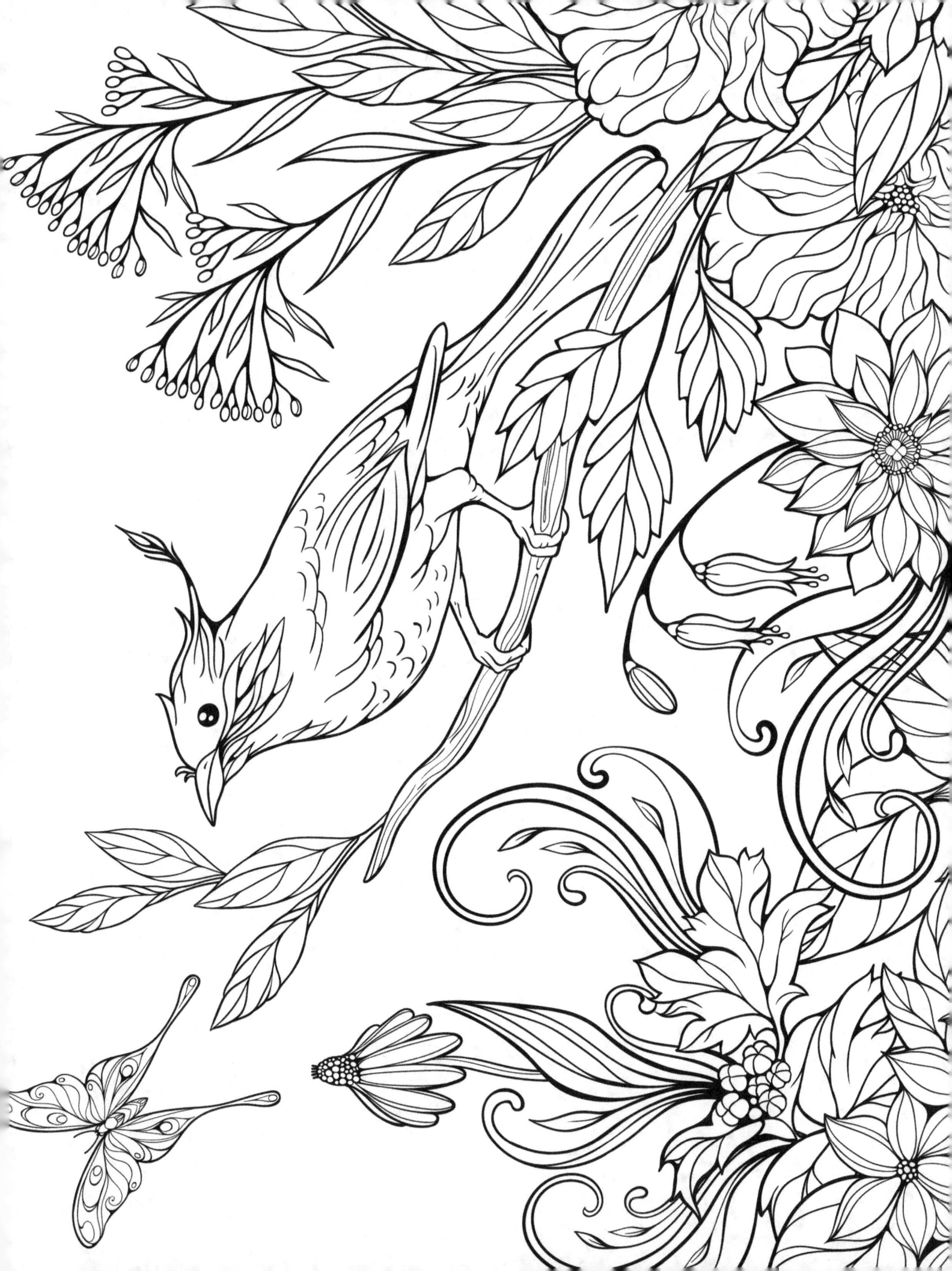

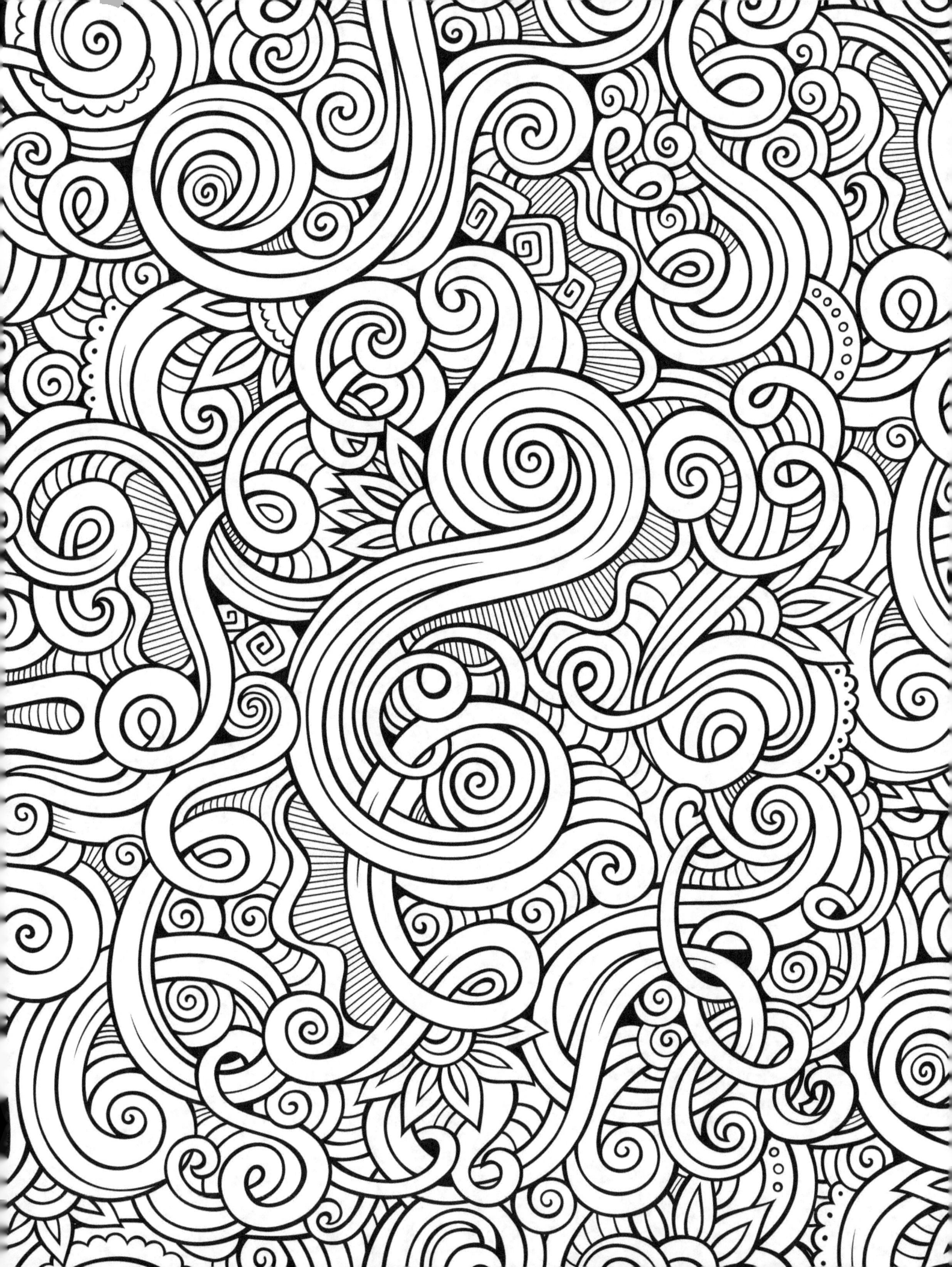

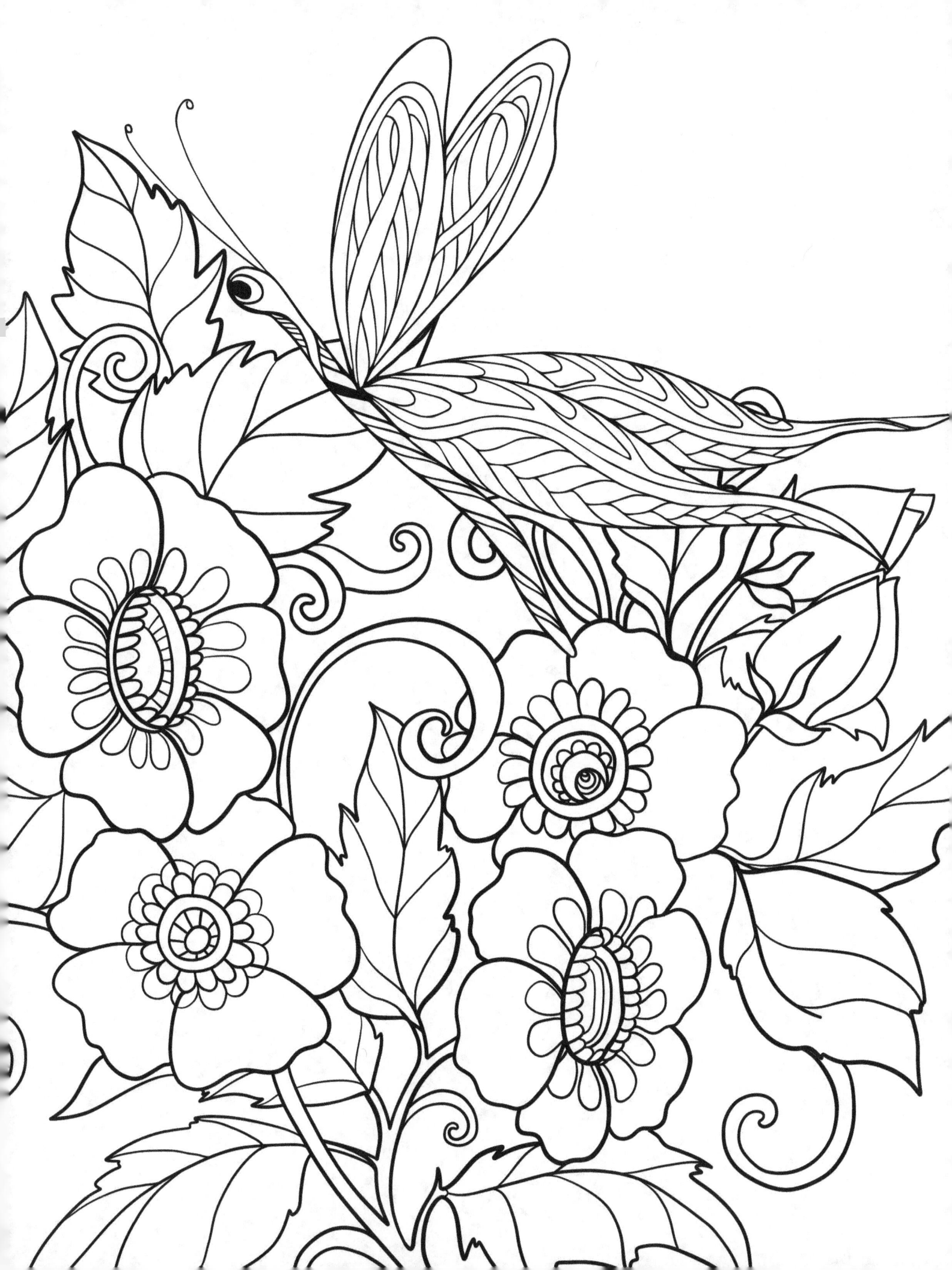

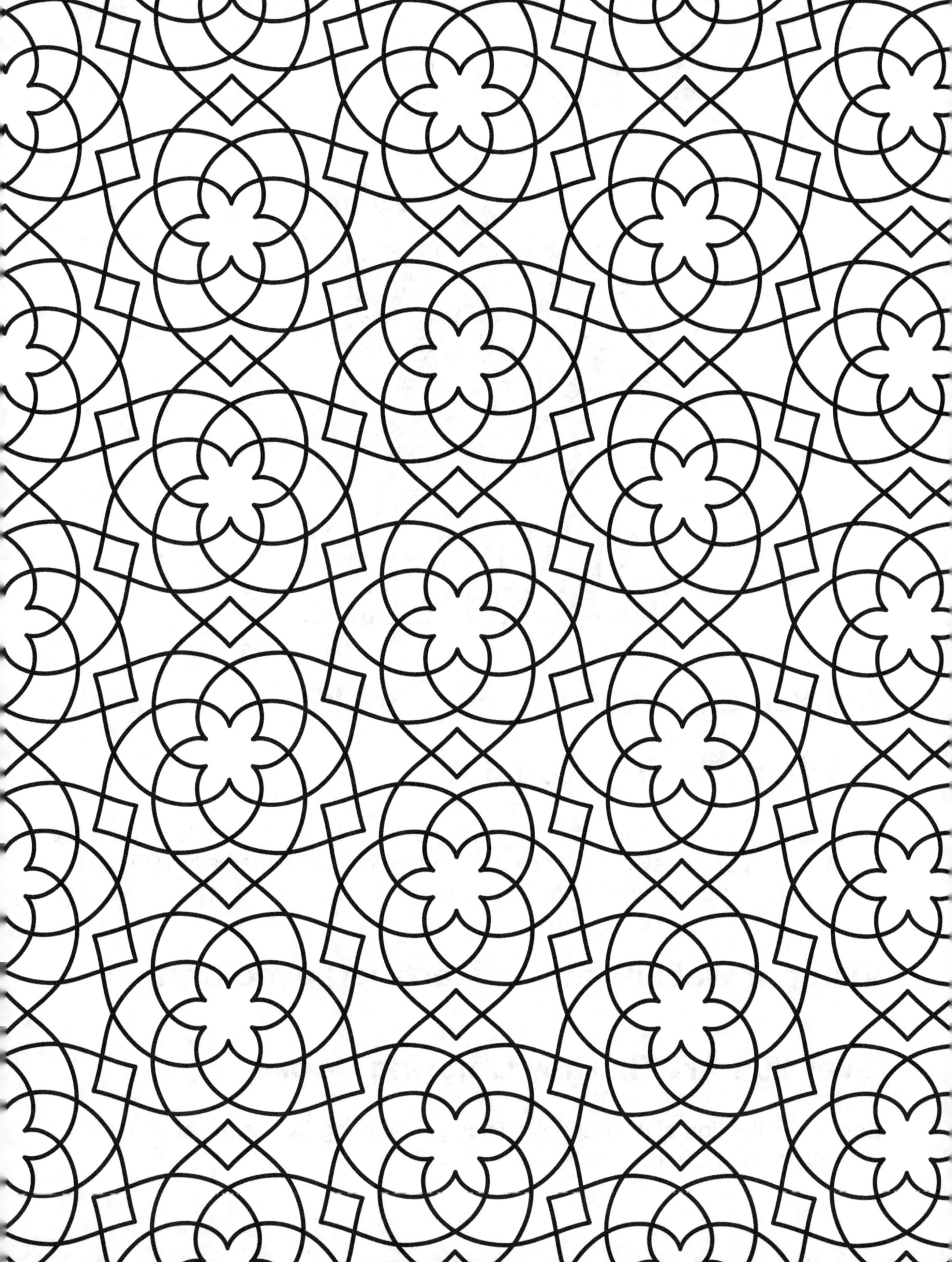

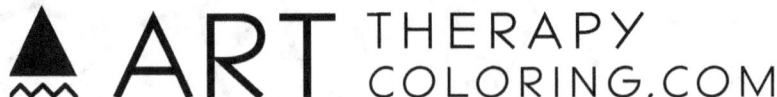

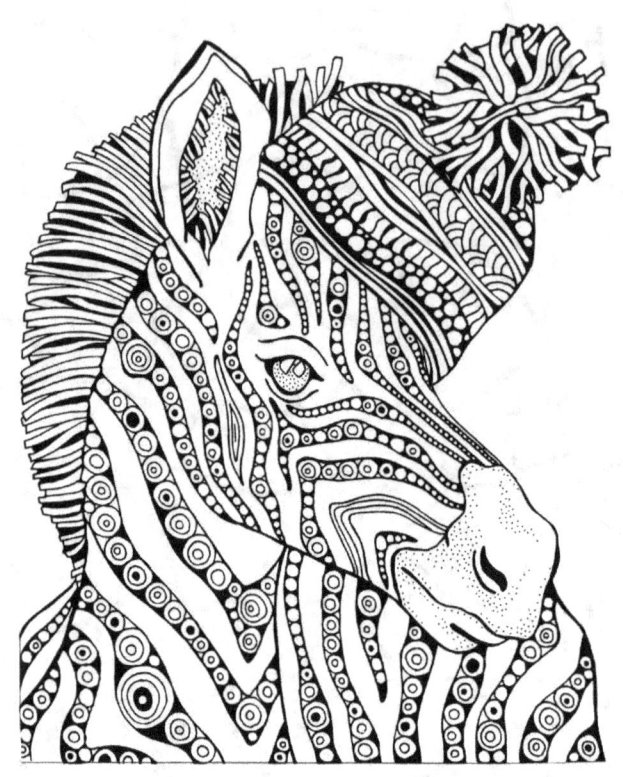

Did You Enjoy Our Coloring Book?

We Want To Hear About It!

Help spread the word about our coloring books! The best way to spread the word is through reviews. We know how busy you are, especially with all of that coloring, but we would appreciate it!

Visit our website at www.arttherapycoloring.com

Over 200 Art Therapy Coloring Books

See our collection of over 200 Art Therapy Coloring Books for Adults, Men, Women, Seniors, Teens, Kids, Boys, and Girls.

Coloring Books For Girls

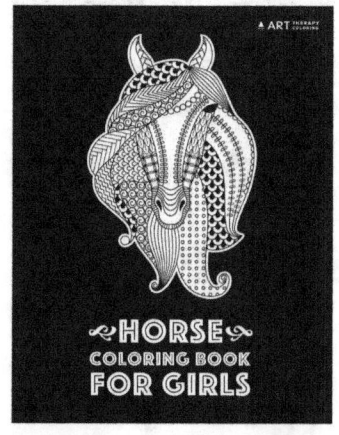

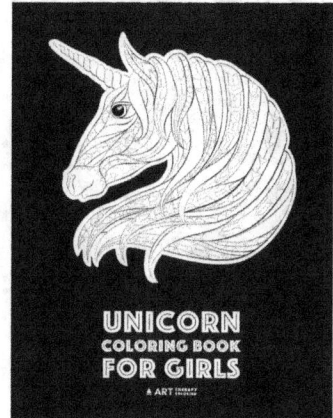

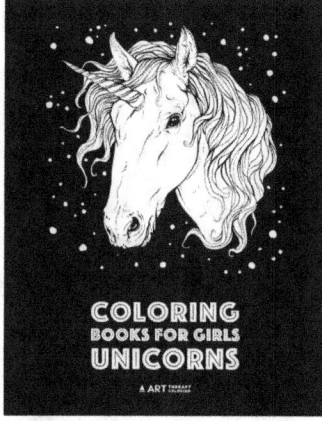

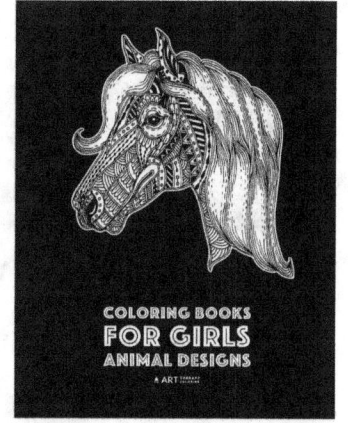

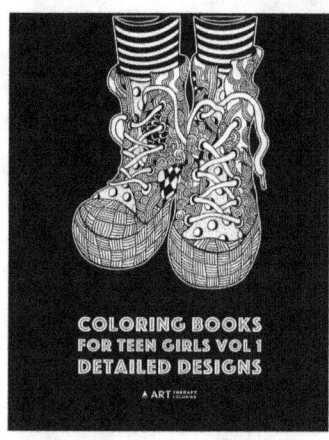

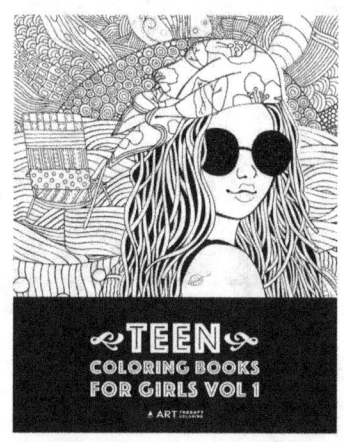

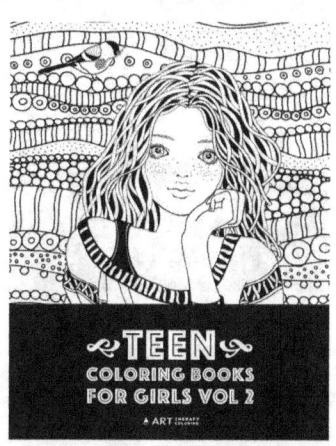

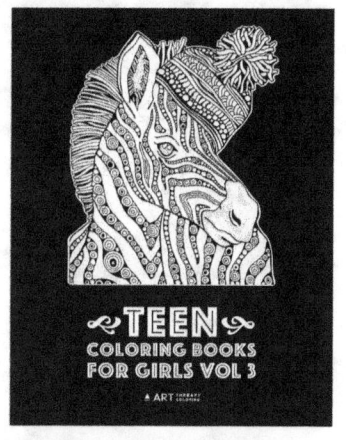

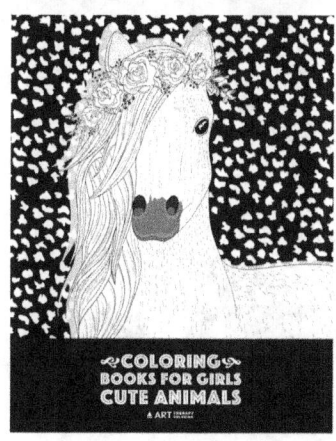

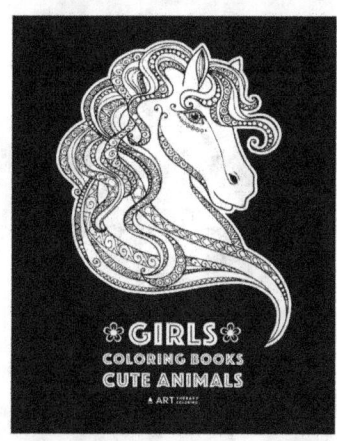

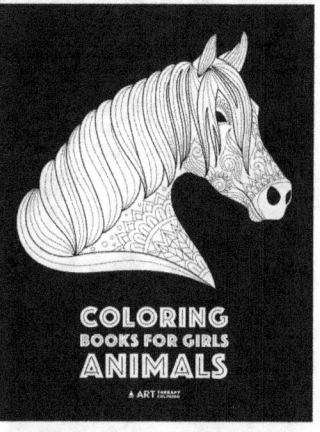

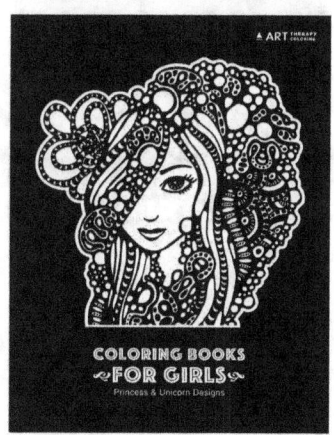

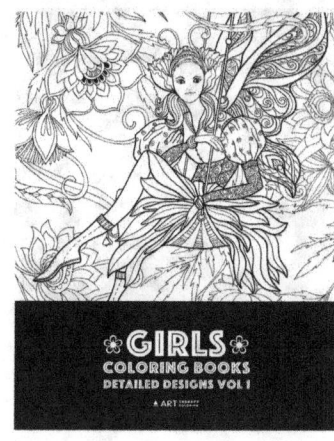

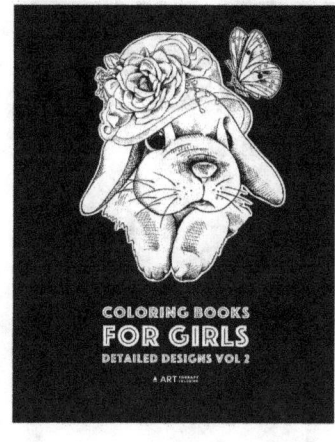

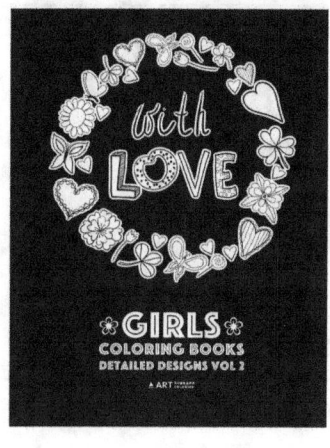

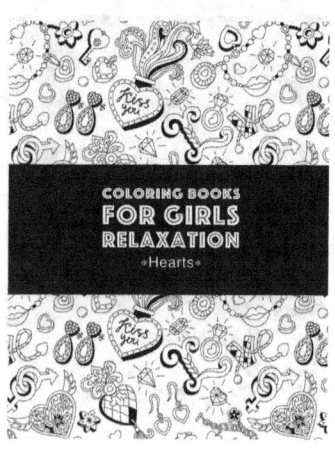

Art Therapy Coloring Books

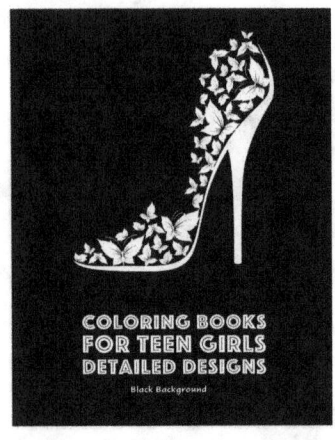

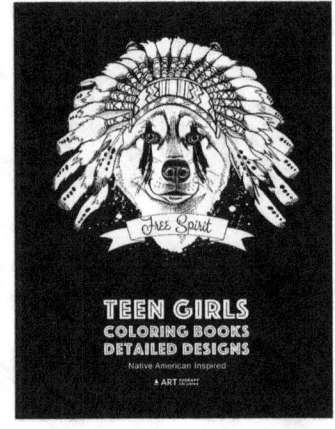

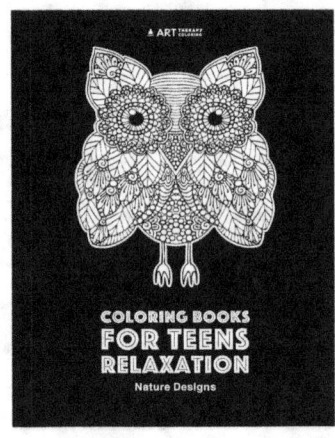

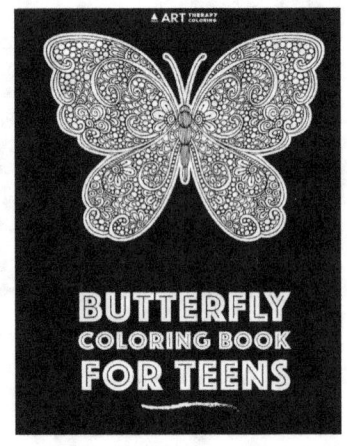

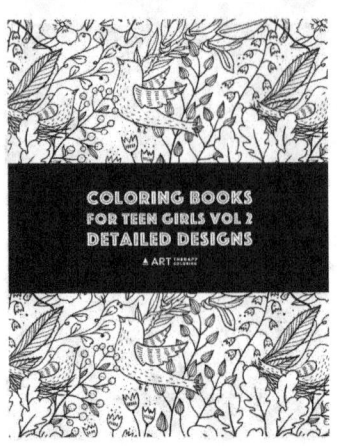

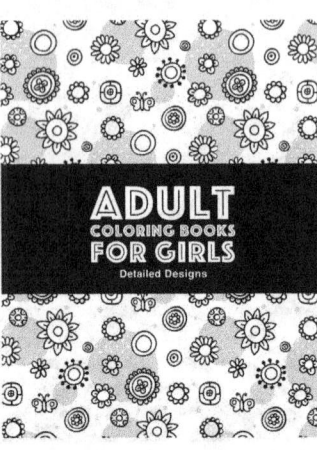

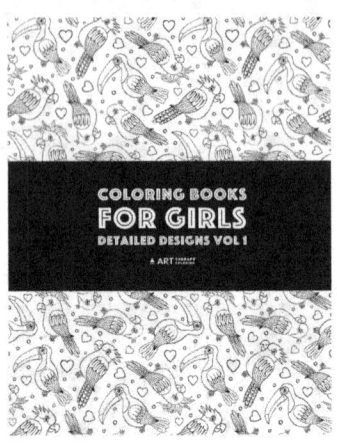

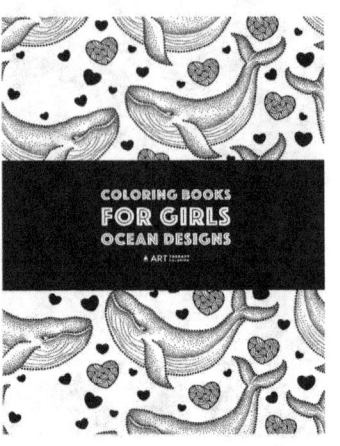

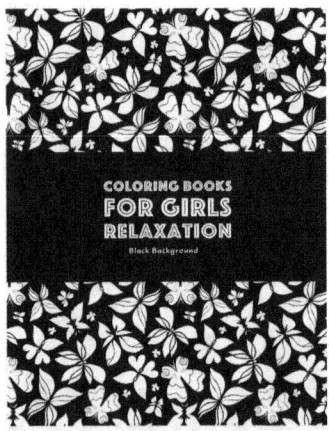

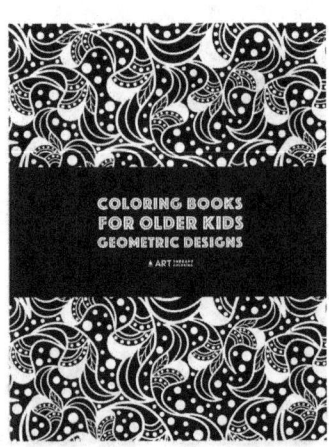

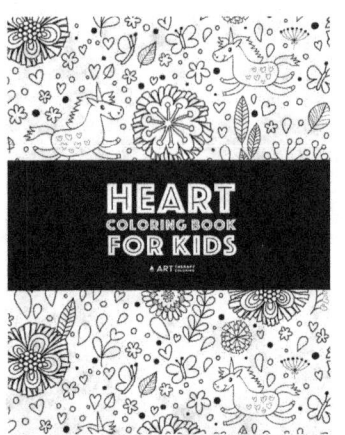

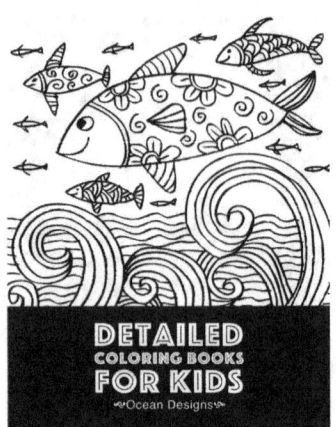

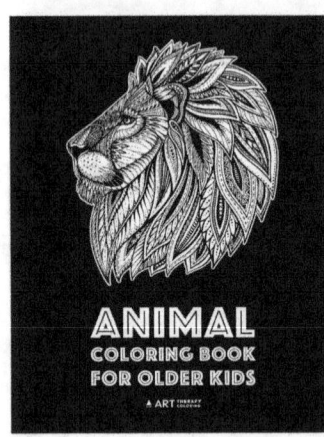

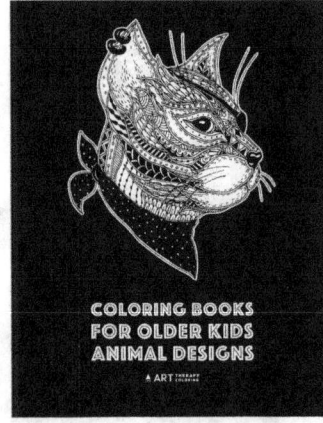

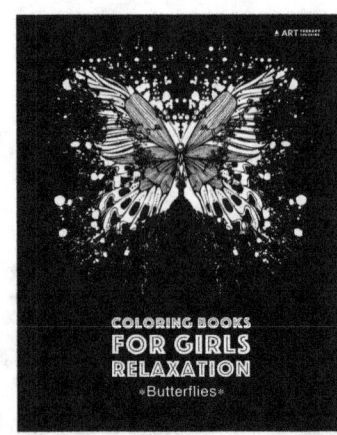

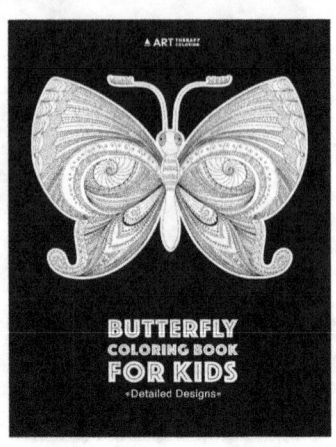

Coloring Books For Kids

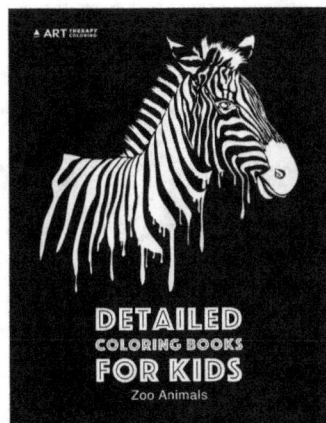

DETAILED COLORING BOOKS FOR KIDS
Zoo Animals

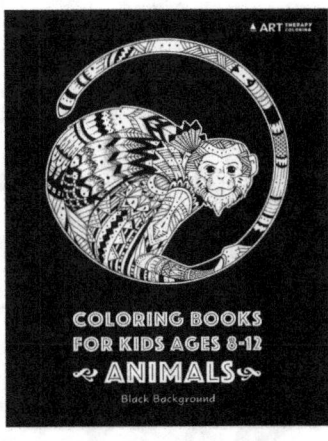

COLORING BOOKS FOR KIDS AGES 8-12 ANIMALS
Black Background

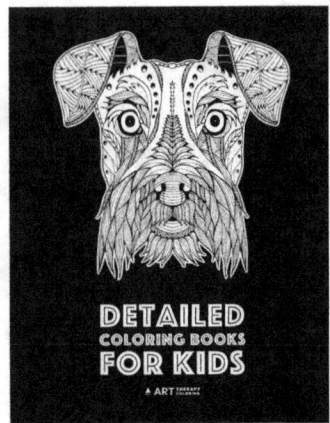

DETAILED COLORING BOOKS FOR KIDS

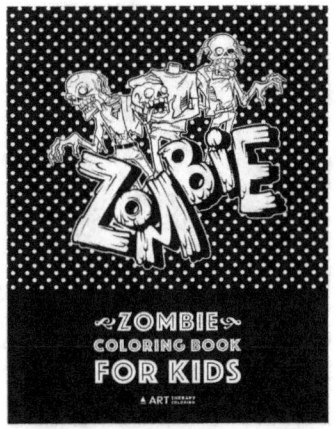

ZOMBIE COLORING BOOK FOR KIDS

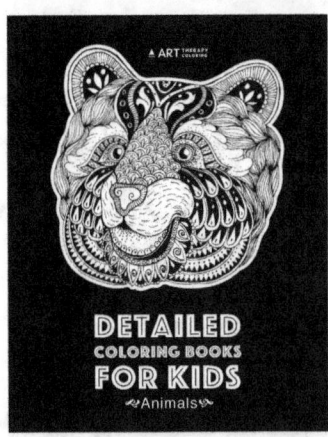

DETAILED COLORING BOOKS FOR KIDS
Animals

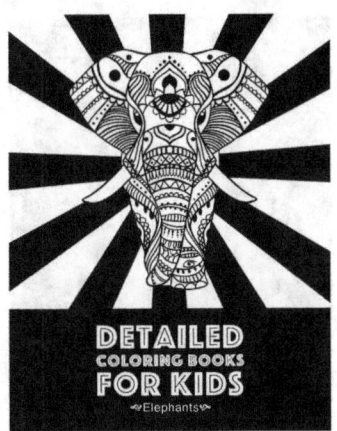

DETAILED COLORING BOOKS FOR KIDS
Elephants

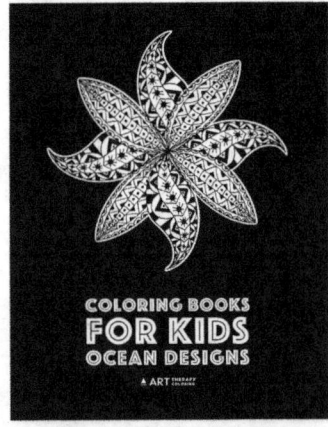

COLORING BOOKS FOR KIDS OCEAN DESIGNS

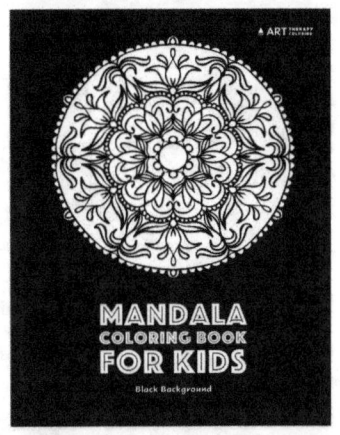

MANDALA COLORING BOOK FOR KIDS
Black Background

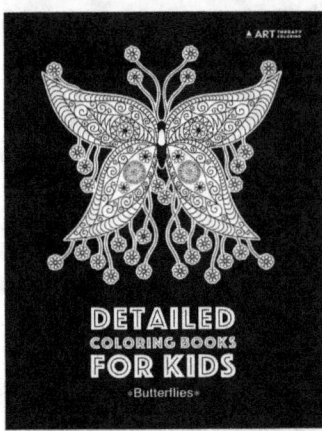

DETAILED COLORING BOOKS FOR KIDS
Butterflies

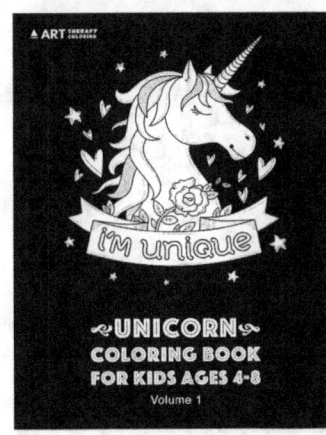

UNICORN COLORING BOOK FOR KIDS AGES 4-8
Volume 1

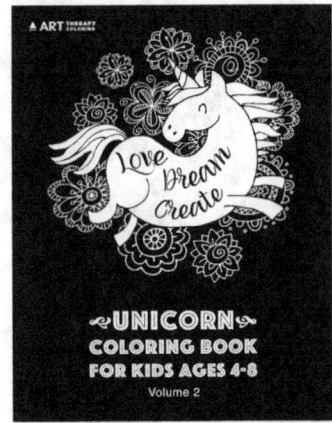

UNICORN COLORING BOOK FOR KIDS AGES 4-8
Volume 2

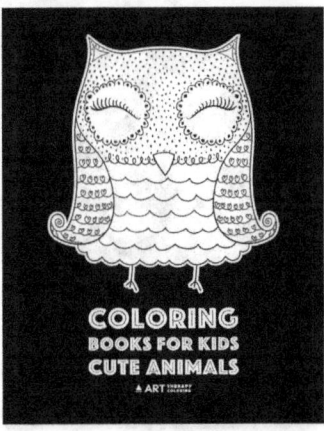

COLORING BOOKS FOR KIDS CUTE ANIMALS

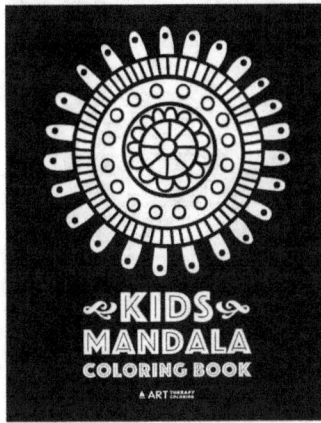

KIDS MANDALA COLORING BOOK

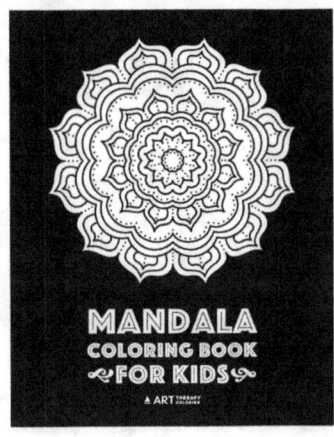

MANDALA COLORING BOOK FOR KIDS

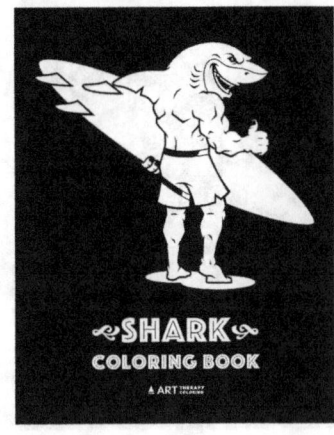

SHARK COLORING BOOK

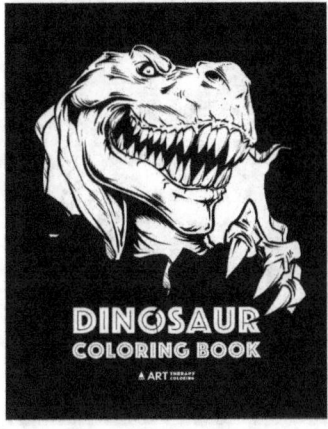

DINOSAUR COLORING BOOK

Coloring Books For Boys

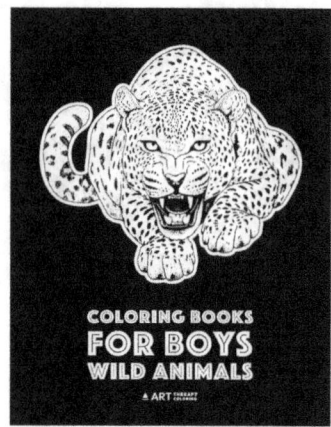

COLORING BOOKS
FOR BOYS
WILD ANIMALS
ART THERAPY COLORING

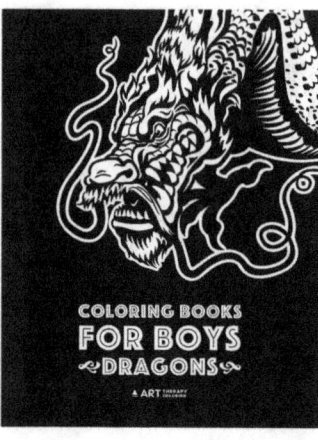

COLORING BOOKS
FOR BOYS
DRAGONS
ART THERAPY COLORING

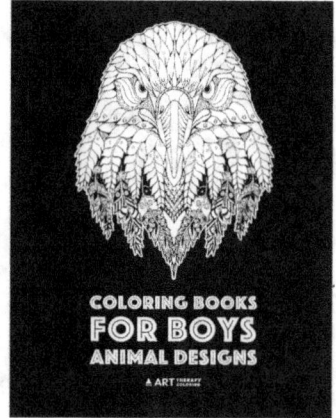

COLORING BOOKS
FOR BOYS
ANIMAL DESIGNS
ART THERAPY COLORING

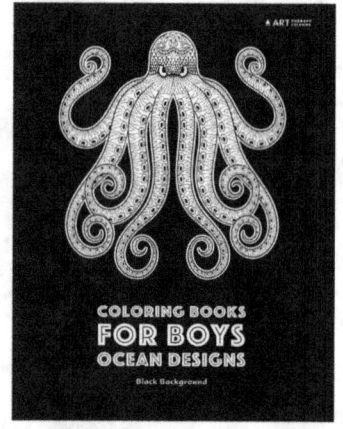

COLORING BOOKS
FOR BOYS
OCEAN DESIGNS
Black Background

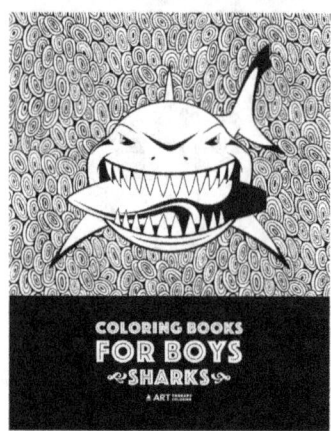

COLORING BOOKS
FOR BOYS
SHARKS
ART THERAPY COLORING

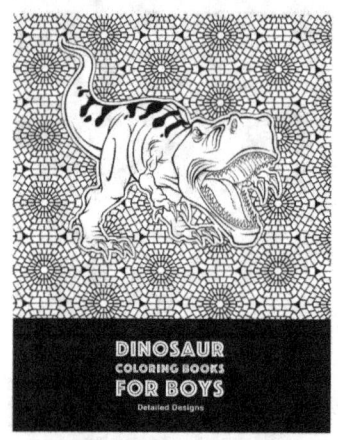

DINOSAUR
COLORING BOOKS
FOR BOYS
Detailed Designs

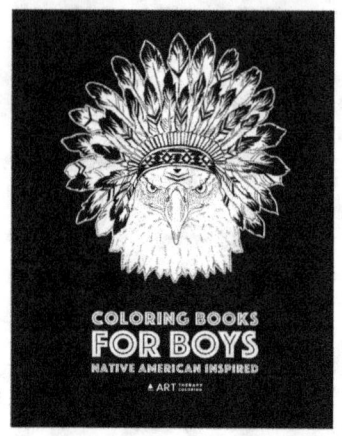

COLORING BOOKS
FOR BOYS
NATIVE AMERICAN INSPIRED
ART THERAPY COLORING

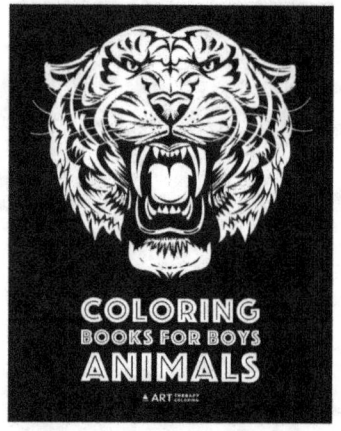

COLORING
BOOKS FOR BOYS
ANIMALS
ART THERAPY COLORING

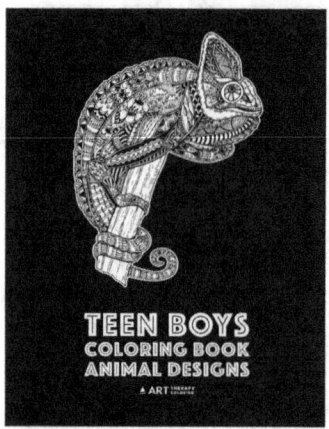

TEEN BOYS
COLORING BOOK
ANIMAL DESIGNS
ART THERAPY COLORING

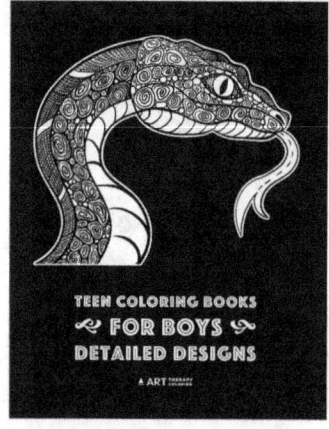

TEEN COLORING BOOKS
FOR BOYS
DETAILED DESIGNS
ART THERAPY COLORING

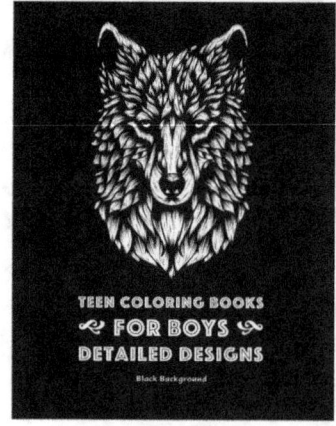

TEEN COLORING BOOKS
FOR BOYS
DETAILED DESIGNS
Black Background

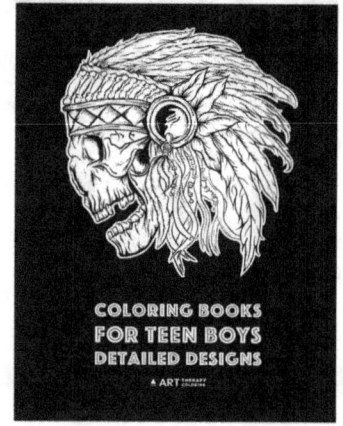

COLORING BOOKS
FOR TEEN BOYS
DETAILED DESIGNS
ART THERAPY COLORING

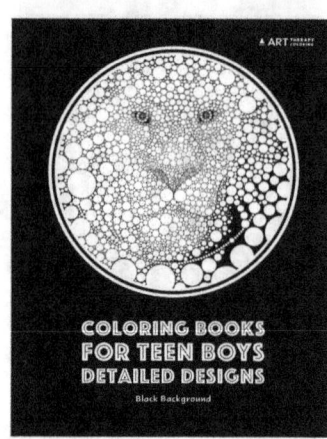

COLORING BOOKS
FOR TEEN BOYS
DETAILED DESIGNS
Black Background

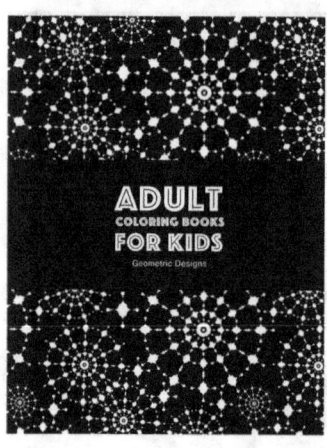

ADULT
COLORING BOOKS
FOR KIDS
Geometric Designs

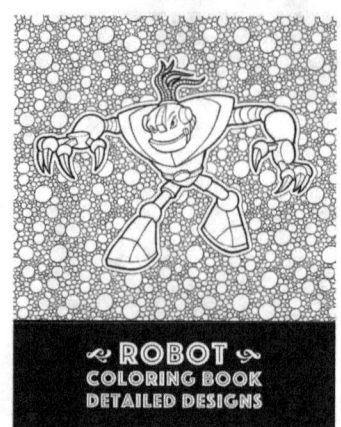

ROBOT
COLORING BOOK
DETAILED DESIGNS

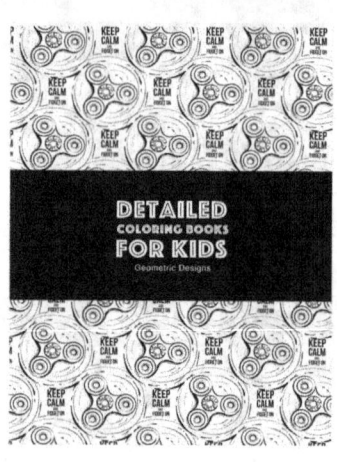

DETAILED
COLORING BOOKS
FOR KIDS
Geometric Designs

Coloring Books For Teens

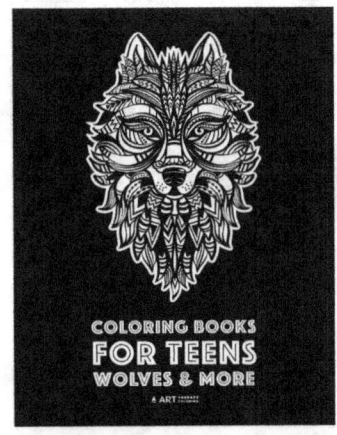

COLORING BOOKS FOR TEENS WOLVES & MORE

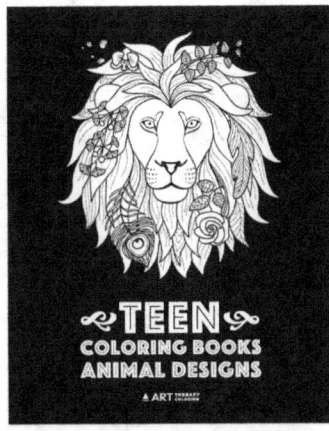

TEEN COLORING BOOKS ANIMAL DESIGNS

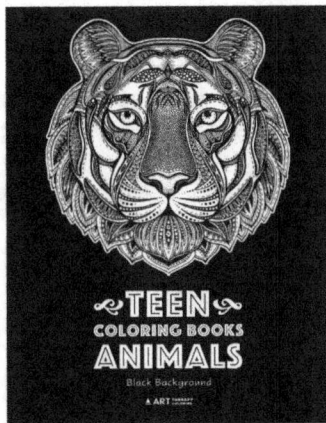

TEEN COLORING BOOKS ANIMALS Black Background

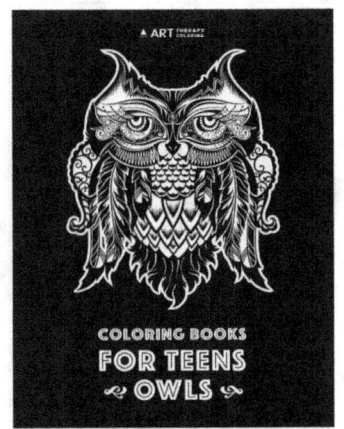

COLORING BOOKS FOR TEENS OWLS

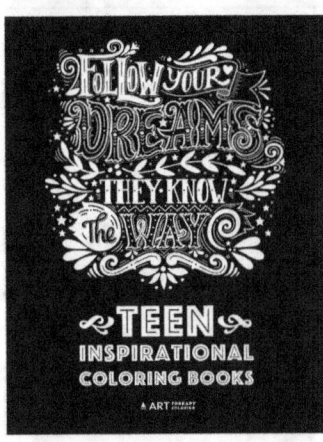

TEEN INSPIRATIONAL COLORING BOOKS

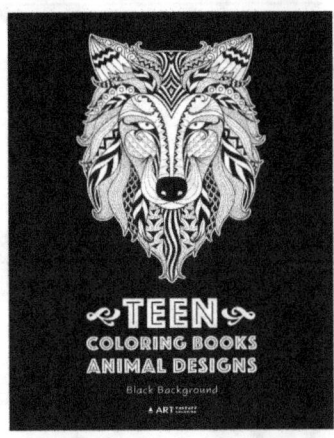

TEEN COLORING BOOKS ANIMAL DESIGNS Black Background

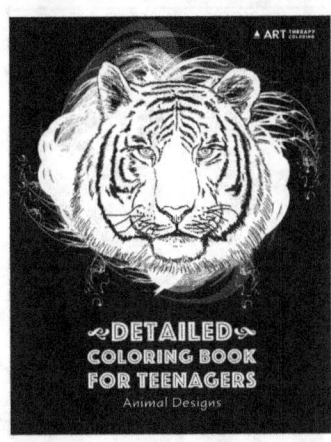

DETAILED COLORING BOOK FOR TEENAGERS Animal Designs

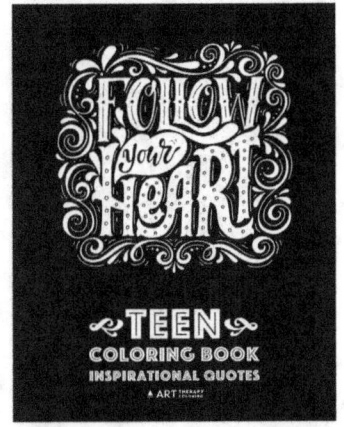

TEEN COLORING BOOK INSPIRATIONAL QUOTES

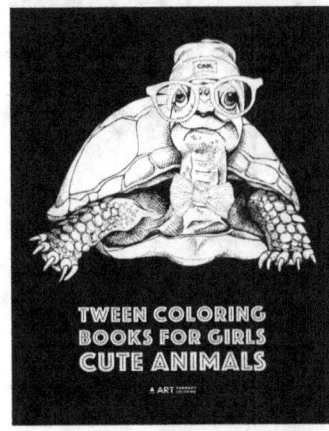

TWEEN COLORING BOOKS FOR GIRLS CUTE ANIMALS

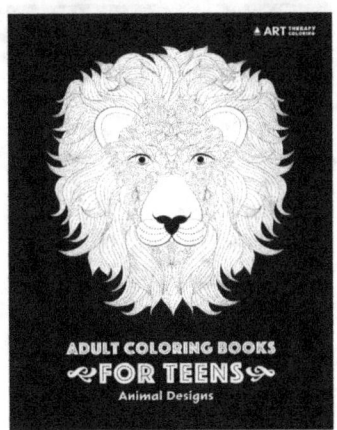

ADULT COLORING BOOKS FOR TEENS Animal Designs

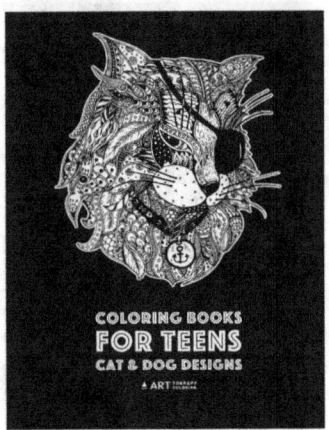

COLORING BOOKS FOR TEENS CAT & DOG DESIGNS

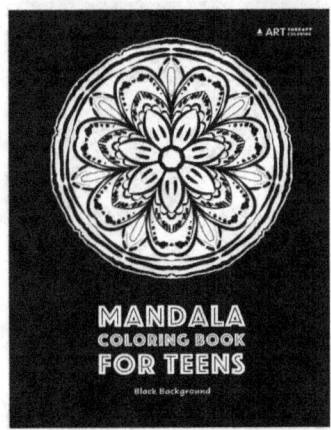

MANDALA COLORING BOOK FOR TEENS Black Background

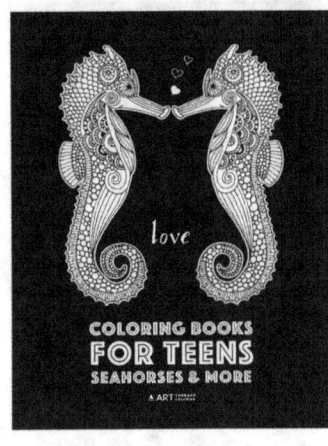

COLORING BOOKS FOR TEENS SEAHORSES & MORE

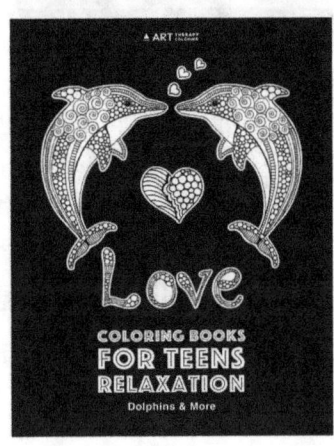

COLORING BOOKS FOR TEENS RELAXATION Dolphins & More

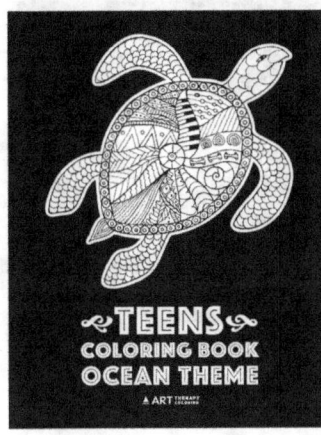

TEENS COLORING BOOK OCEAN THEME

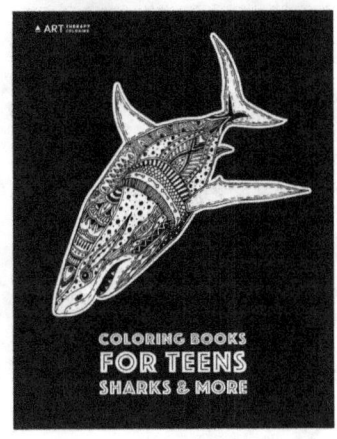

COLORING BOOKS FOR TEENS SHARKS & MORE

Coloring Books For Teens

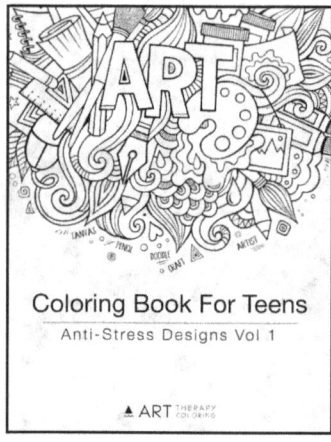

Coloring Book For Teens
Anti-Stress Designs Vol 1

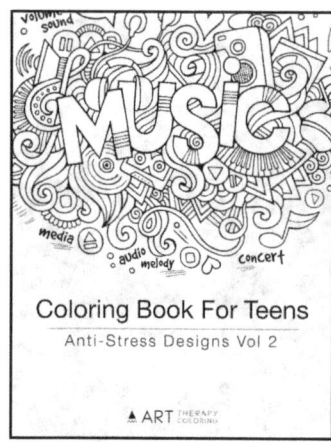

Coloring Book For Teens
Anti-Stress Designs Vol 2

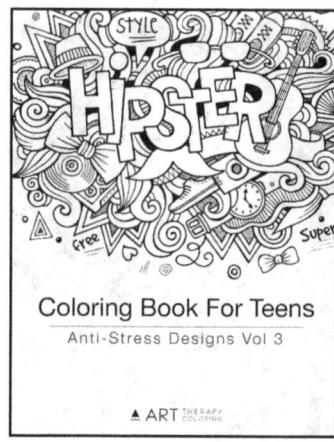

Coloring Book For Teens
Anti-Stress Designs Vol 3

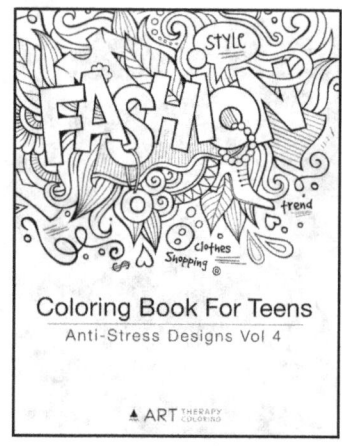

Coloring Book For Teens
Anti-Stress Designs Vol 4

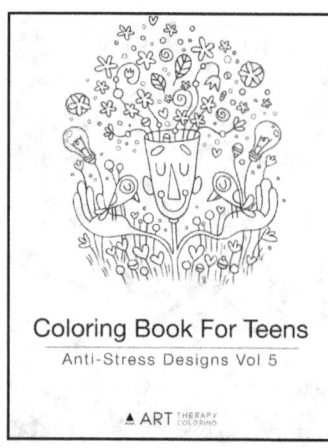

Coloring Book For Teens
Anti-Stress Designs Vol 5

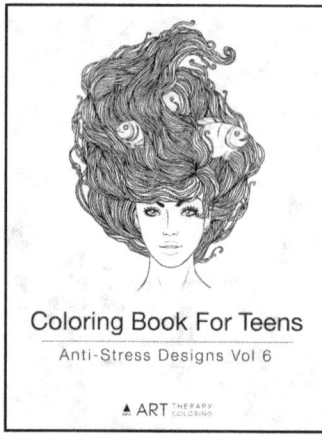

Coloring Book For Teens
Anti-Stress Designs Vol 6

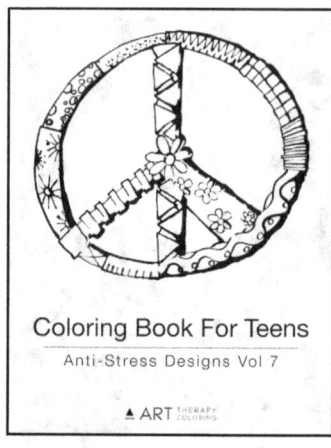

Coloring Book For Teens
Anti-Stress Designs Vol 7

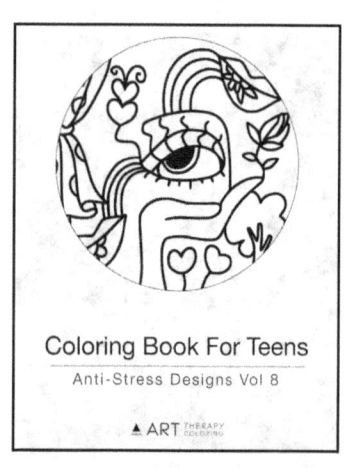

Coloring Book For Teens
Anti-Stress Designs Vol 8

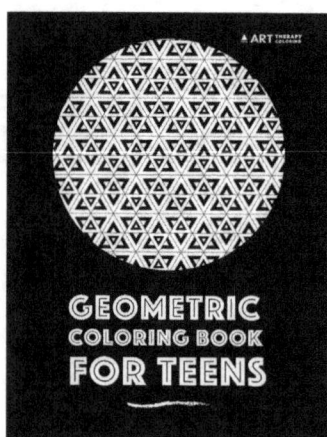

GEOMETRIC COLORING BOOK FOR TEENS

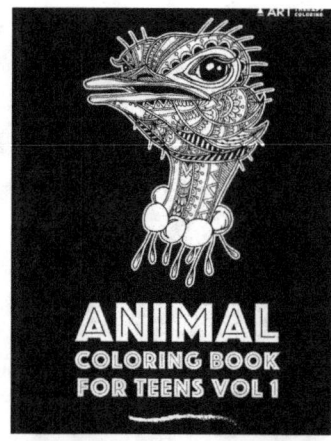

ANIMAL COLORING BOOK FOR TEENS VOL 1

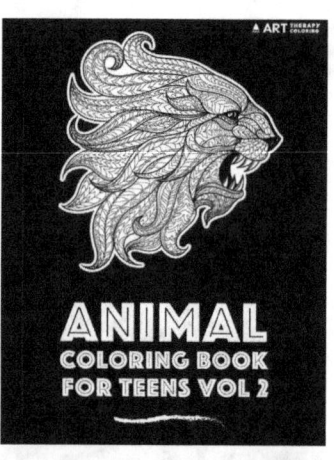

ANIMAL COLORING BOOK FOR TEENS VOL 2

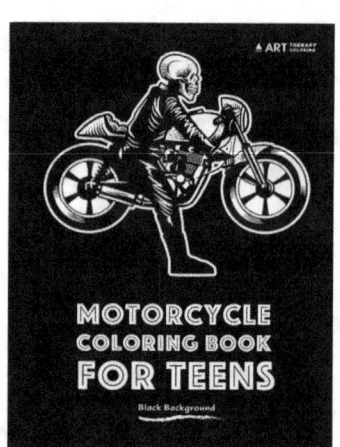

MOTORCYCLE COLORING BOOK FOR TEENS
Black Background

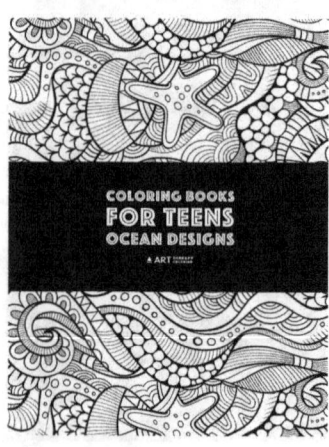

COLORING BOOKS FOR TEENS OCEAN DESIGNS

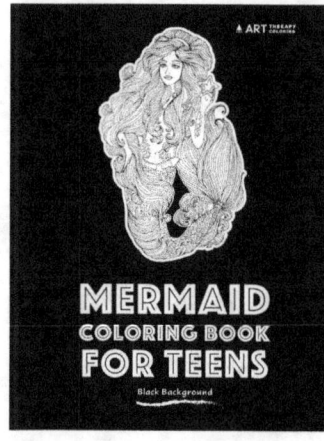

MERMAID COLORING BOOK FOR TEENS
Black Background

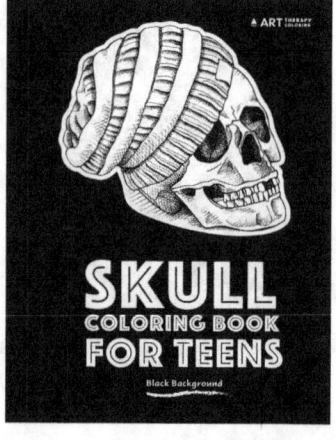

SKULL COLORING BOOK FOR TEENS
Black Background

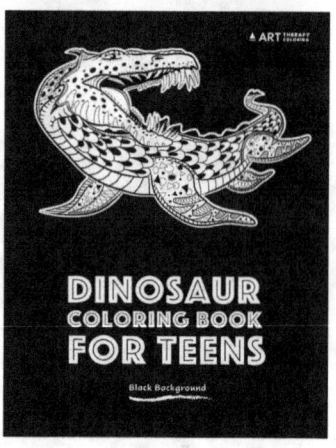

DINOSAUR COLORING BOOK FOR TEENS
Black Background

Coloring Books For Adults

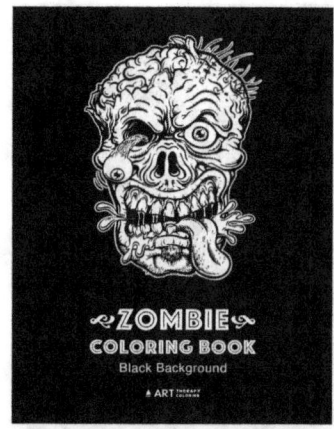

ZOMBIE
COLORING BOOK
Black Background

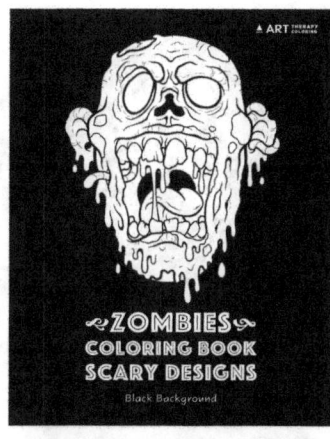

ZOMBIES
COLORING BOOK
SCARY DESIGNS
Black Background

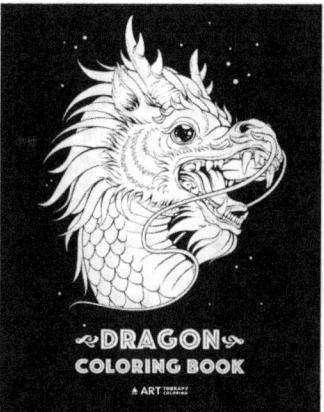

DRAGON
COLORING BOOK

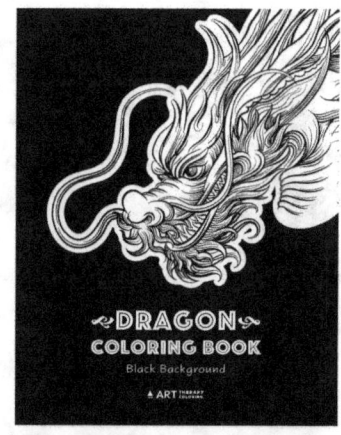

DRAGON
COLORING BOOK
Black Background

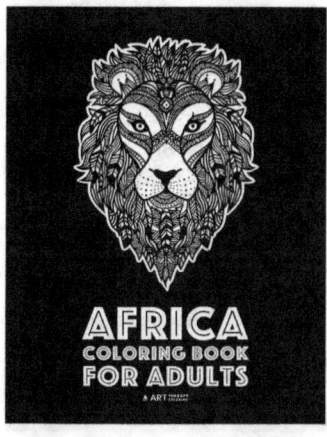

AFRICA
COLORING BOOK
FOR ADULTS

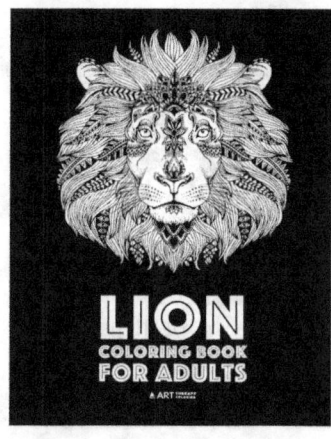

LION
COLORING BOOK
FOR ADULTS

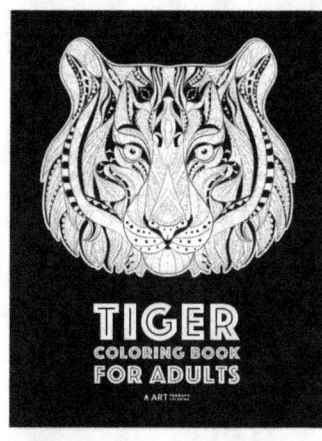

TIGER
COLORING BOOK
FOR ADULTS

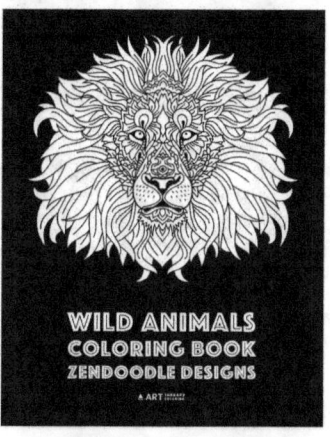

WILD ANIMALS
COLORING BOOK
ZENDOODLE DESIGNS

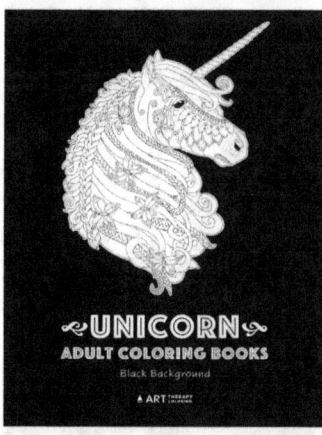

UNICORN
ADULT COLORING BOOKS
Black Background

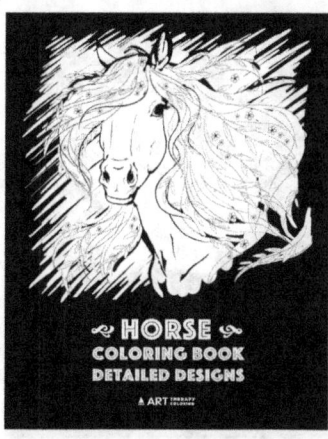

HORSE
COLORING BOOK
DETAILED DESIGNS

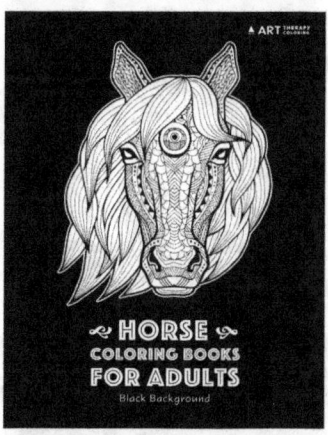

HORSE
COLORING BOOKS
FOR ADULTS
Black Background

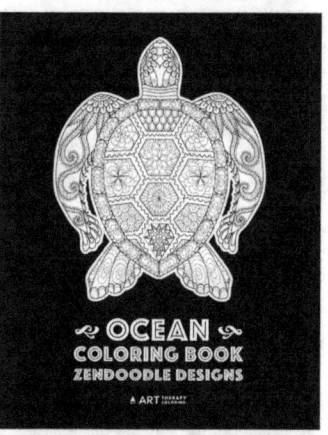

OCEAN
COLORING BOOK
ZENDOODLE DESIGNS

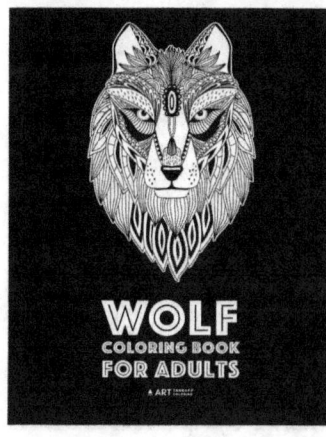

WOLF
COLORING BOOK
FOR ADULTS

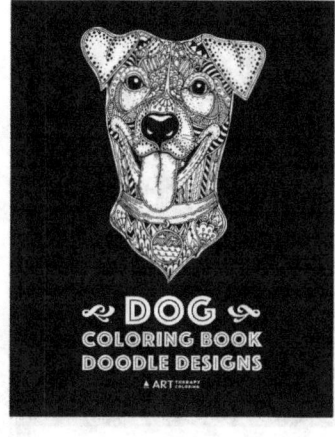

DOG
COLORING BOOK
DOODLE DESIGNS

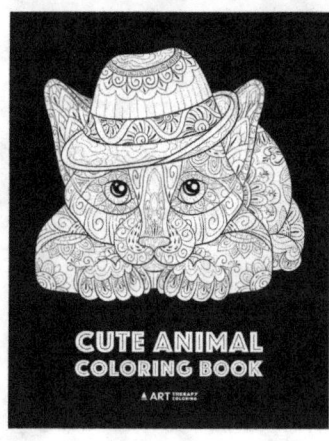

CUTE ANIMAL
COLORING BOOK

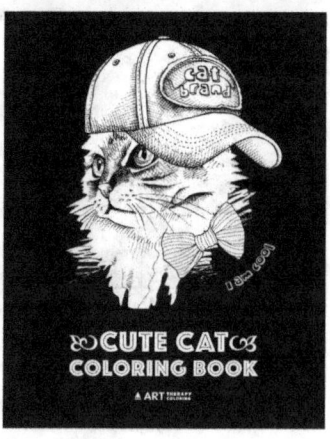

CUTE CAT
COLORING BOOK

Coloring Books For Adults

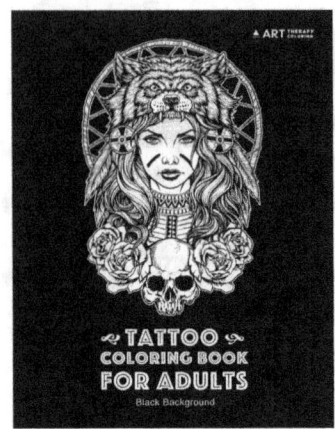

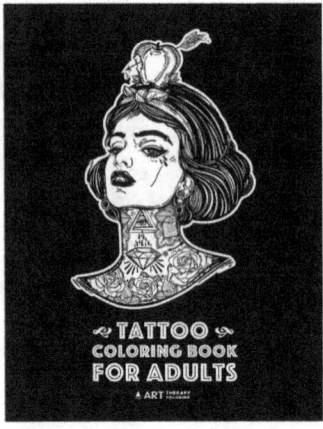

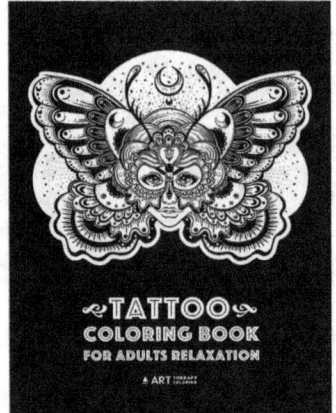

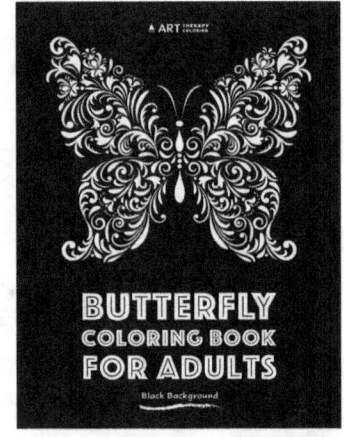

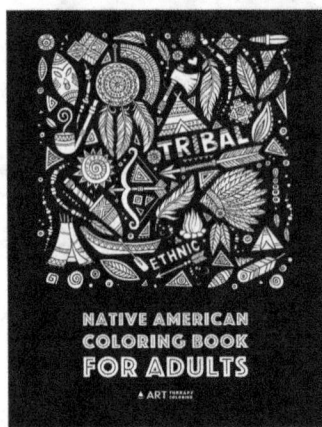

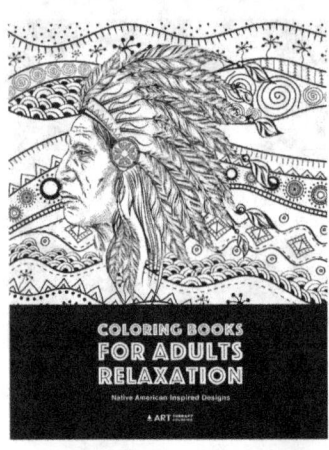

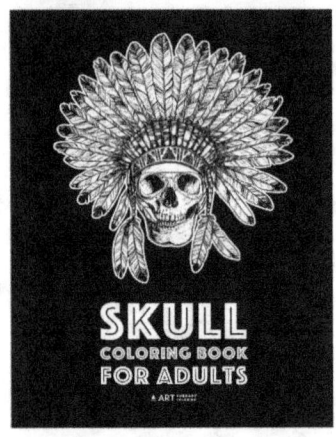

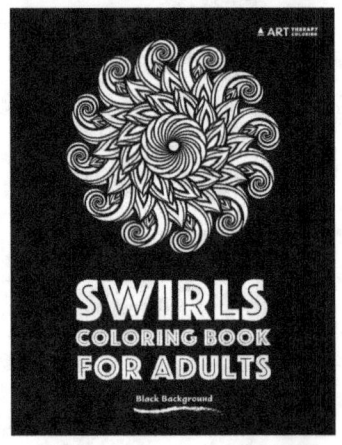

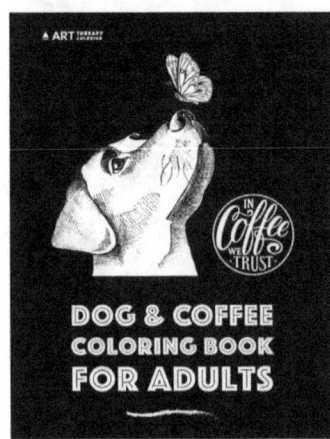

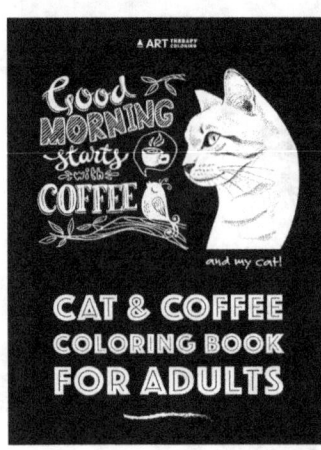

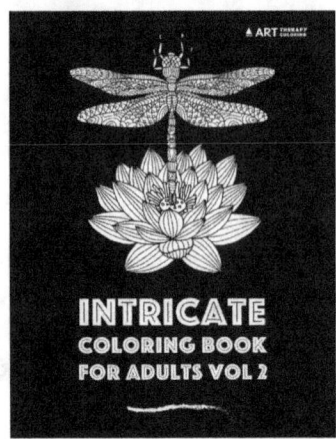

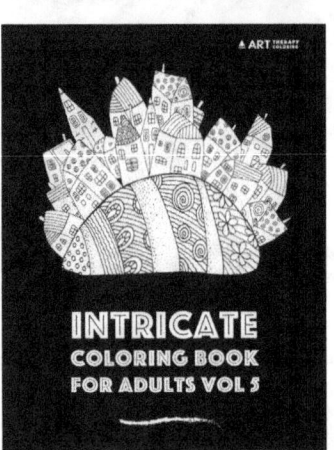

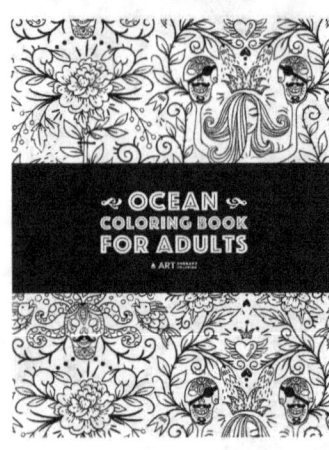

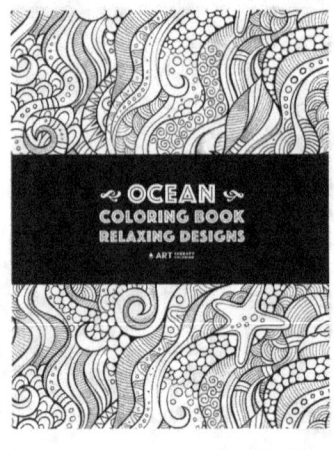

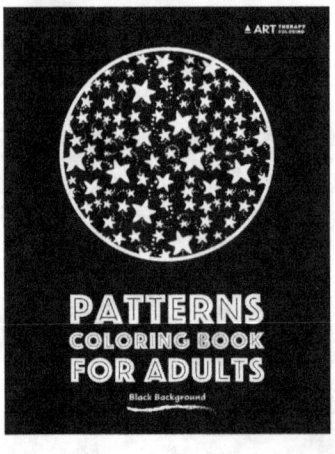

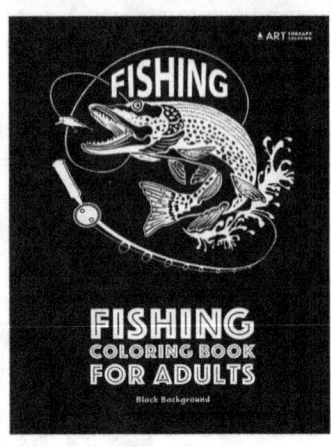

Coloring Books For Adults

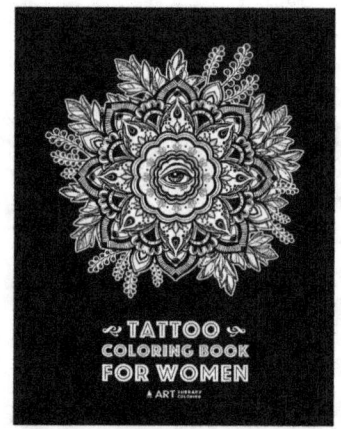

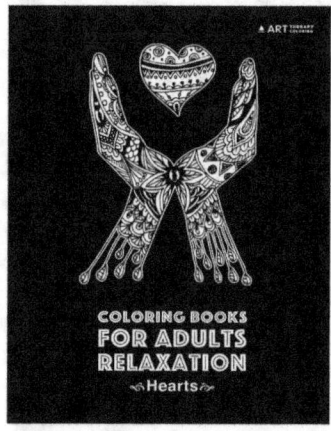

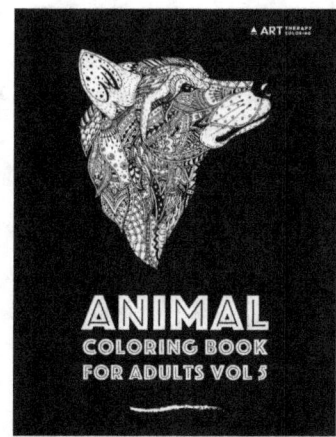

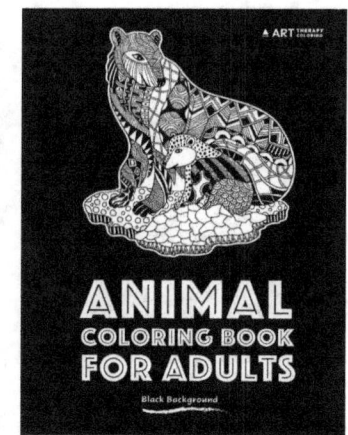

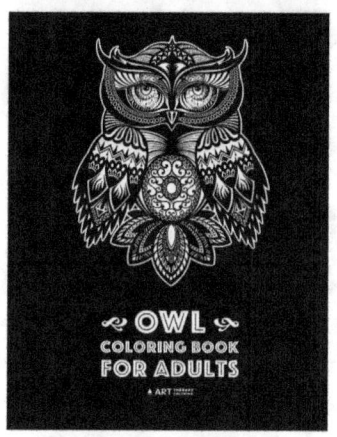

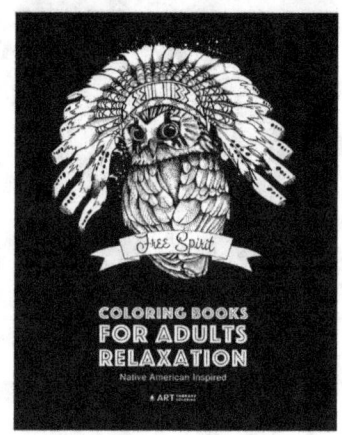

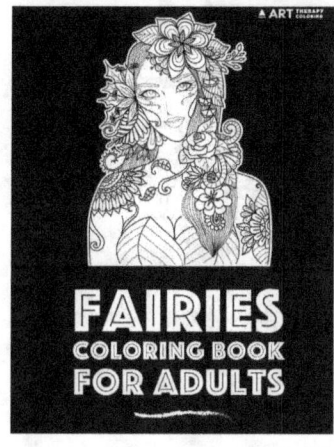

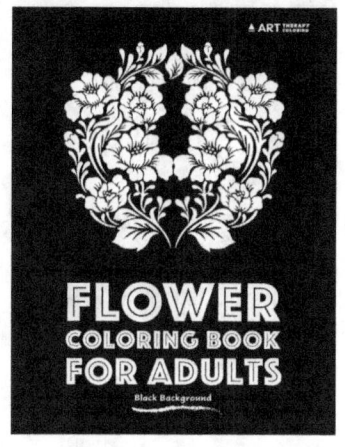

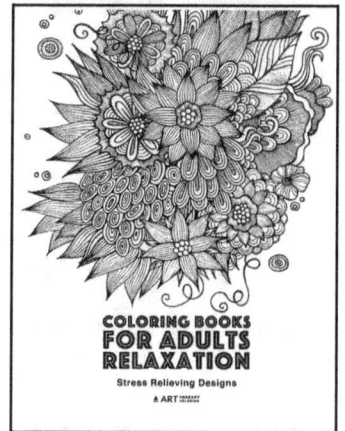

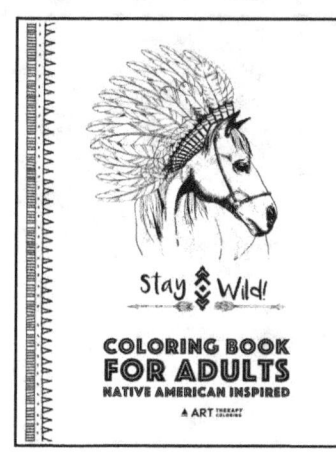

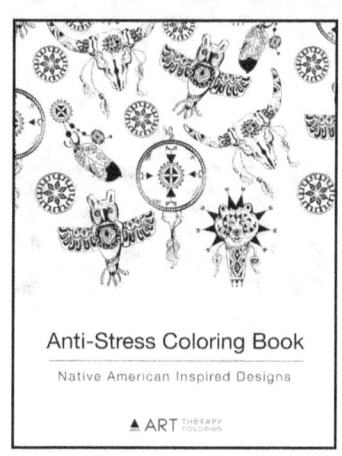

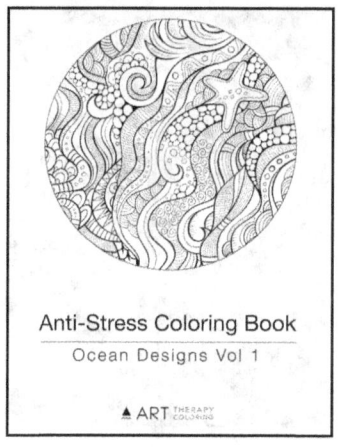

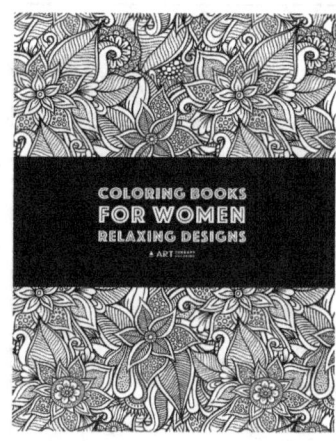

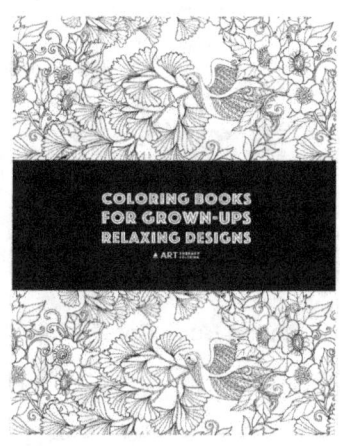

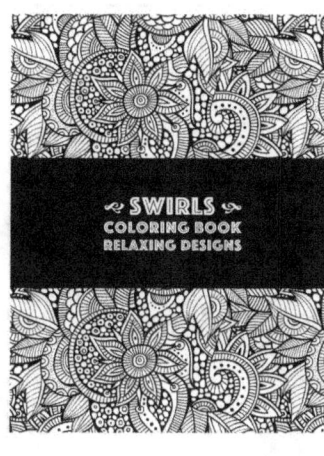

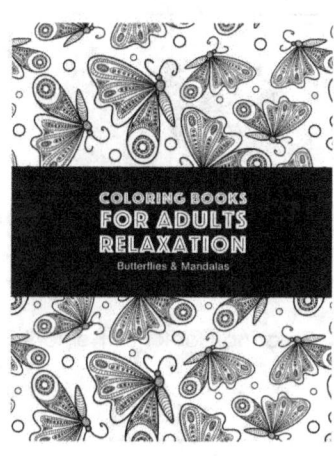

Coloring Books For Seniors

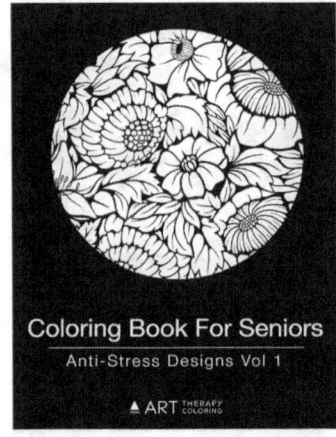

Coloring Book For Seniors
Anti-Stress Designs Vol 1

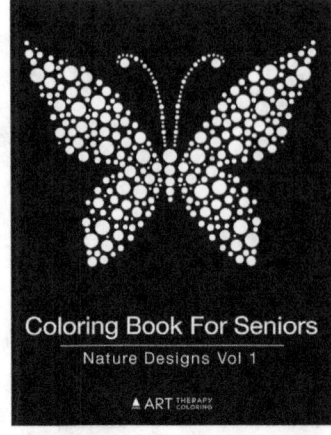

Coloring Book For Seniors
Nature Designs Vol 1

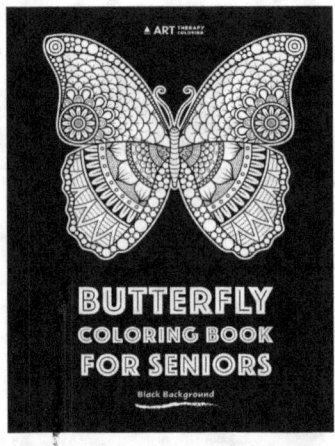

BUTTERFLY COLORING BOOK FOR SENIORS
Black Background

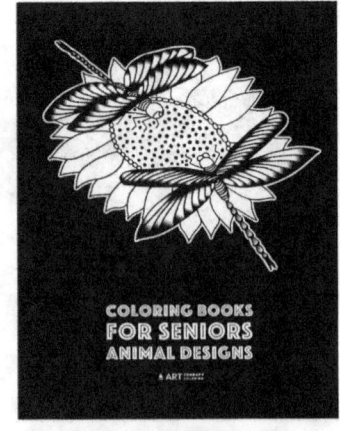

COLORING BOOKS FOR SENIORS ANIMAL DESIGNS

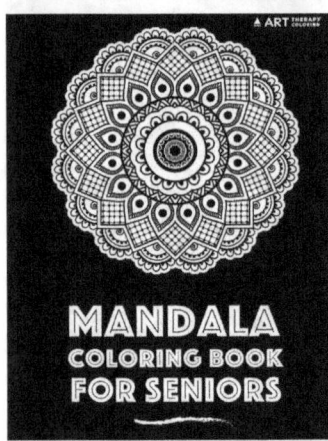

MANDALA COLORING BOOK FOR SENIORS

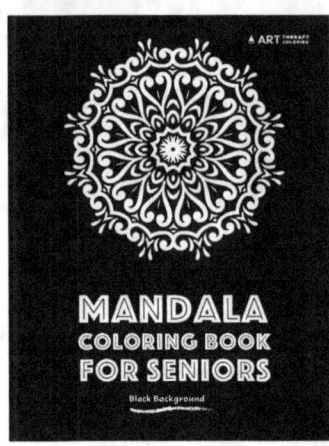

MANDALA COLORING BOOK FOR SENIORS
Black Background

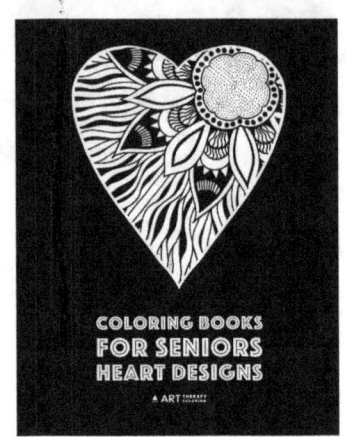

COLORING BOOKS FOR SENIORS HEART DESIGNS

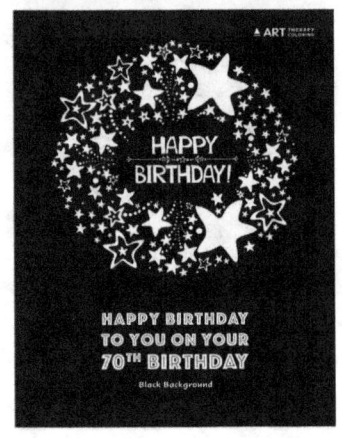

HAPPY BIRTHDAY TO YOU ON YOUR 70TH BIRTHDAY
Black Background

COLORING BOOKS FOR SENIORS SWIRL DESIGNS
Black Background

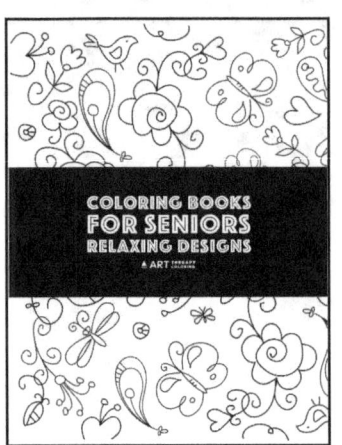

COLORING BOOKS FOR SENIORS RELAXING DESIGNS

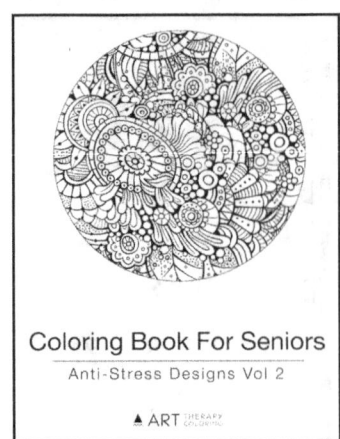

Coloring Book For Seniors
Anti-Stress Designs Vol 2

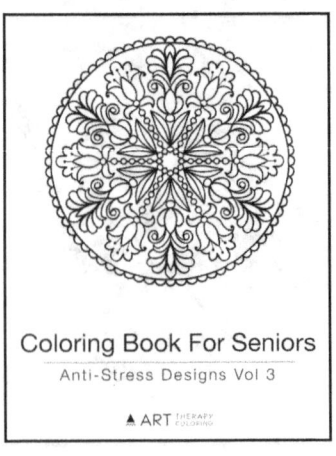

Coloring Book For Seniors
Anti-Stress Designs Vol 3

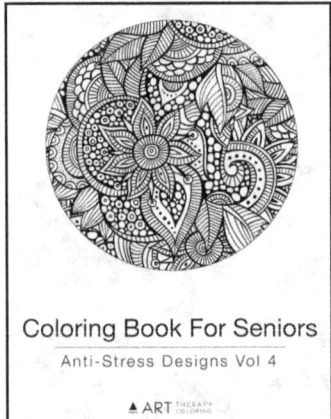

Coloring Book For Seniors
Anti-Stress Designs Vol 4

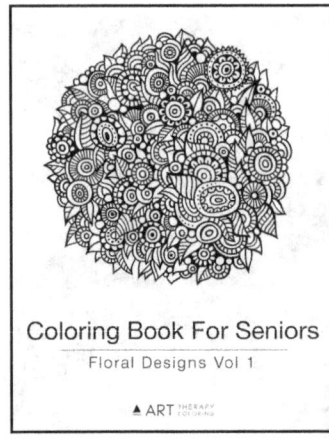

Coloring Book For Seniors
Floral Designs Vol 1

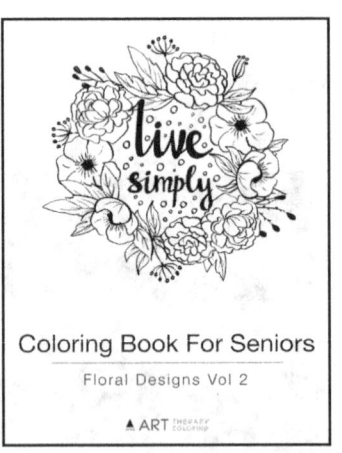

Coloring Book For Seniors
Floral Designs Vol 2

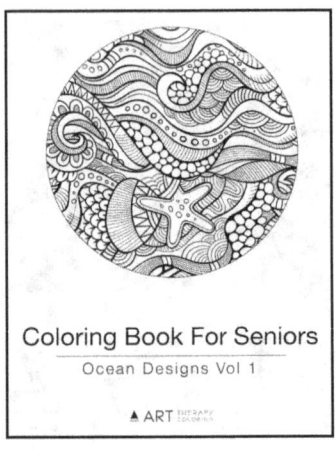

Coloring Book For Seniors
Ocean Designs Vol 1

Coloring Books For Men

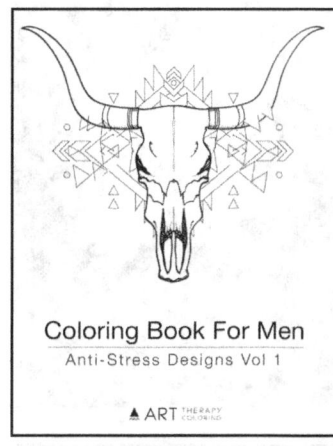

Coloring Book For Men
Anti-Stress Designs Vol 1

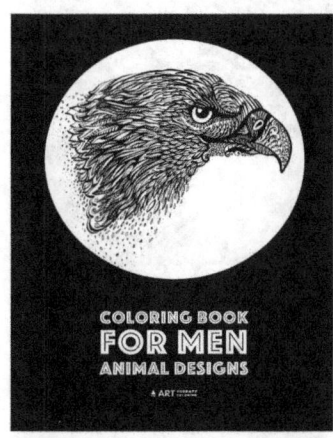

COLORING BOOK
FOR MEN
ANIMAL DESIGNS

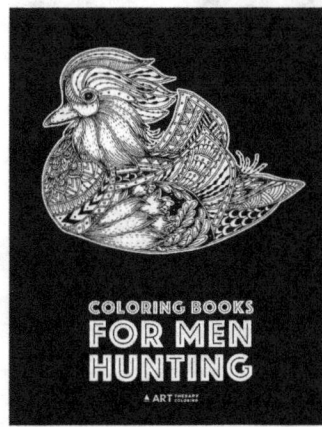

COLORING BOOKS
FOR MEN
HUNTING

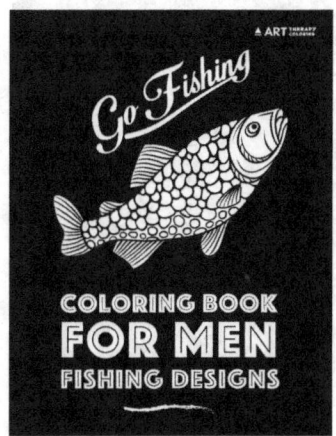

Go Fishing
COLORING BOOK
FOR MEN
FISHING DESIGNS

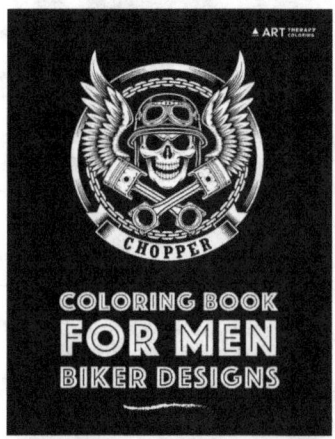

COLORING BOOK
FOR MEN
BIKER DESIGNS

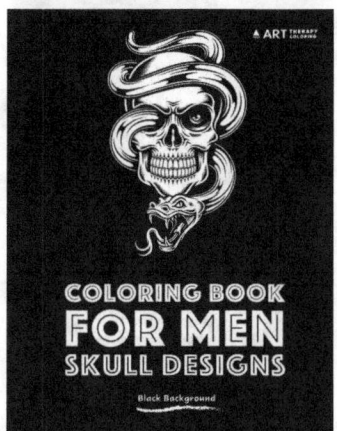

COLORING BOOK
FOR MEN
SKULL DESIGNS
Black Background

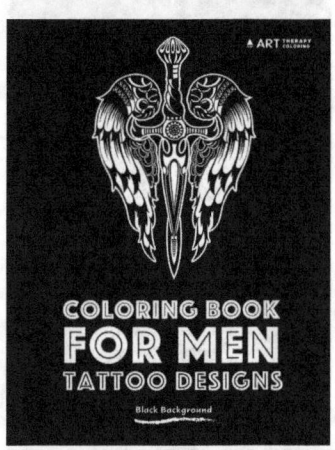

COLORING BOOK
FOR MEN
TATTOO DESIGNS
Black Background

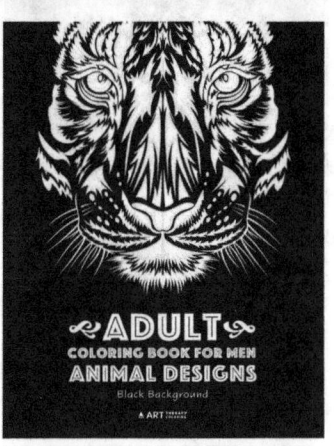

ADULT
COLORING BOOK FOR MEN
ANIMAL DESIGNS
Black Background

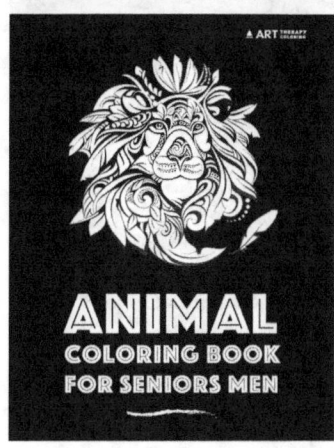

ANIMAL
COLORING BOOK
FOR SENIORS MEN

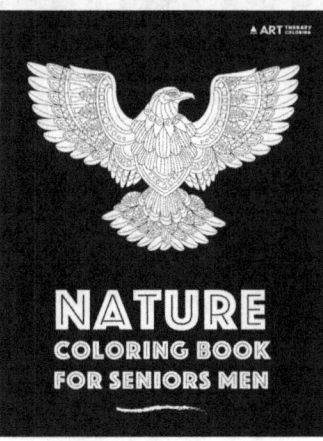

NATURE
COLORING BOOK
FOR SENIORS MEN

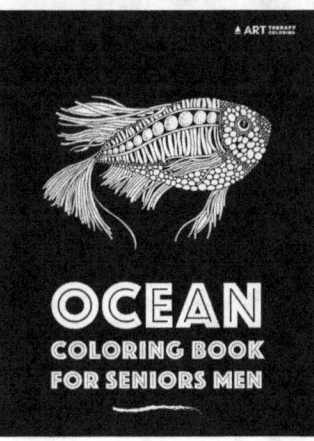

OCEAN
COLORING BOOK
FOR SENIORS MEN

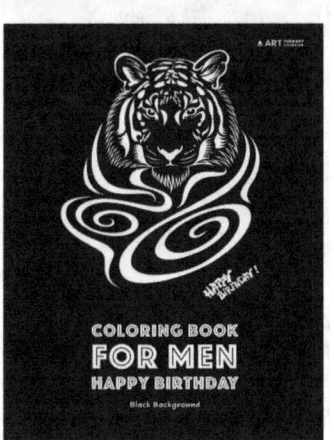

COLORING BOOK
FOR MEN
HAPPY BIRTHDAY
Black Background

Coloring Books For Special Occasions

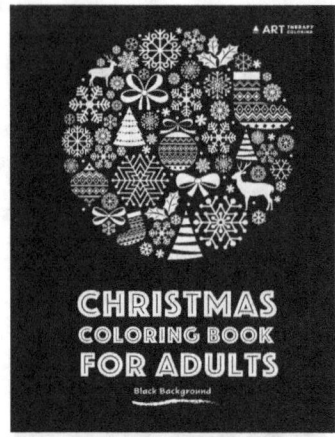

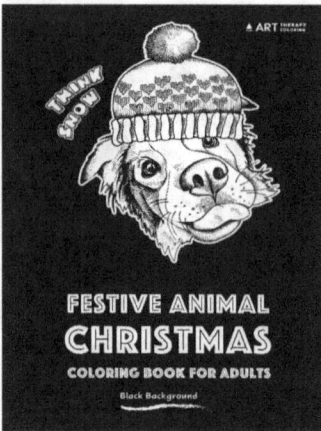

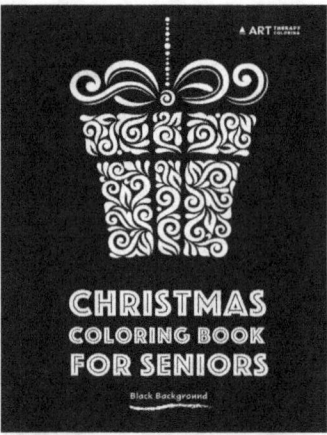

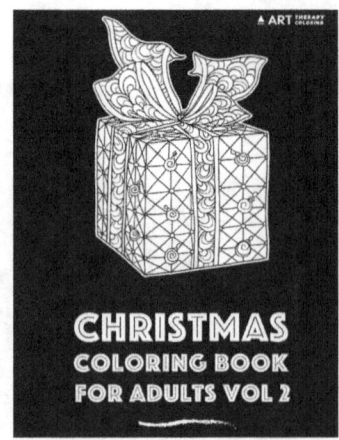

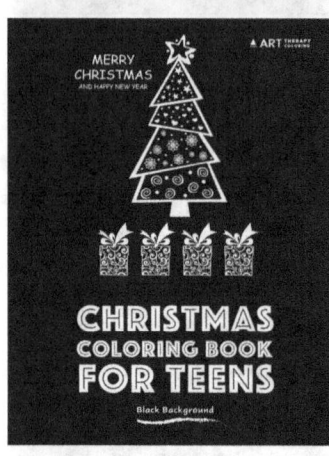

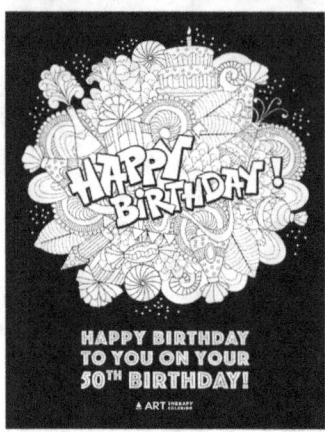

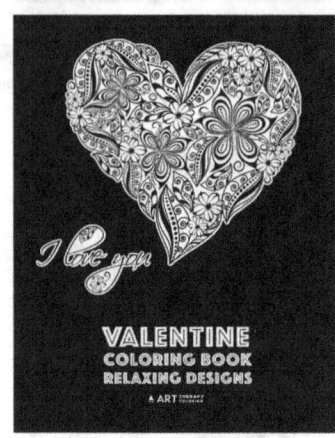

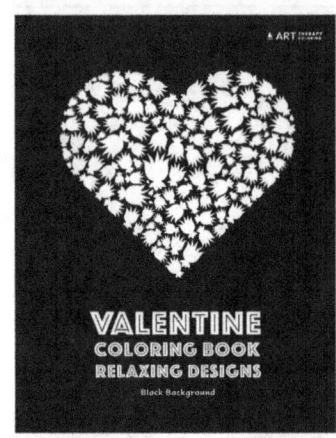

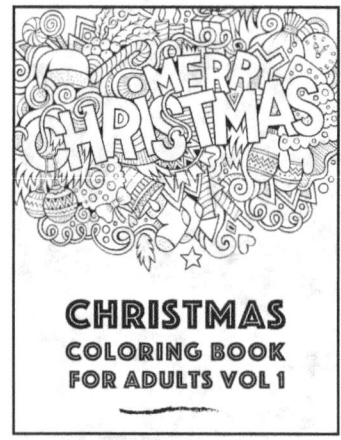

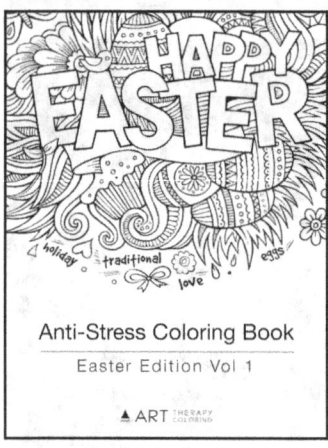

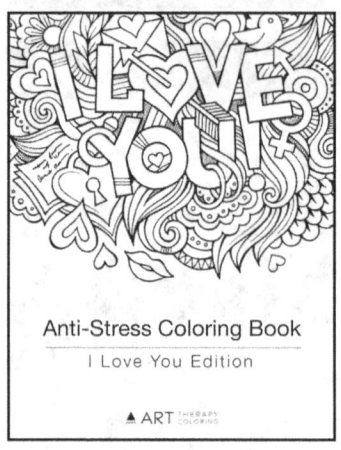

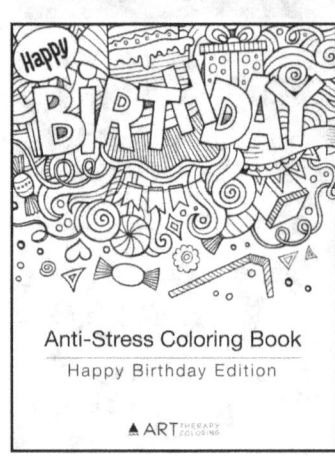

Coloring Books For Teen Girls Vol 2
Detailed Designs

Published by:
Art Therapy Coloring
El Dorado Hills, California
www.arttherapycoloring.com

Shutterstock Images

ISBN: 978-1-64126-039-8

www.ingramcontent.com/pod-product-compliance
Lightning Source LLC
Chambersburg PA
CBHW081343180526

45171CB00006B/592